Why My Third Husband Will Be a Dog

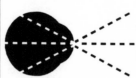

This Large Print Book carries the
Seal of Approval of N.A.V.H.

Why My Third Husband Will Be a Dog

THE AMAZING ADVENTURES OF AN ORDINARY WOMAN

Lisa Scottoline

THORNDIKE PRESS

A part of Gale, Cengage Learning

Detroit • New York • San Francisco • New Haven, Conn • Waterville, Maine • London

GALE
CENGAGE Learning™

LIBRARY OF CONGRESS CATALOGING-IN-PUBLICATION DATA

Scottoline, Lisa.
  Why my third husband will be a dog : the amazing
adventures of an ordinary woman / by Lisa Scottoline.
    p. cm. — (Thorndike Press large print core)
    ISBN-13: 978-1-4104-2322-1 (alk. paper)
    ISBN-10: 1-4104-2322-0 (alk. paper)
    1. Women—Humor. 2. Man-woman relationships—Humor.
3. Women—Life skills guides—Humor. 4. Large type books.
  I. Title.
  PN6231.W6S315 2010
  814'.54—dc22   2009042754

Published in 2010 by arrangement with St. Martin's Press, LLC.

For extraordinary ordinary women
everywhere

PREFACE

I love Eleanor Roosevelt's quote about women being like tea bags. I have it written on a Post-it stuck to my computer and I keep one in my jewelry box, too. The quote is the reason I started writing books, but I'm getting ahead of myself.

Here's the story of me: I'm an English major who became a lawyer, though I always wanted to write a novel. After my first divorce, I found myself single with a young baby (don't try this at home). I wanted to stay home to raise my baby, but I had no dough. My back was against the wall, so I decided to finally try to write that novel. I figured you can't get any broker than broke.

Turns out you can.

I wrote for the next five years, living on credit cards, nursing my baby by day and reading rejection letters by night. Yet it was a deliriously happy time of my life.

7

Women are tea bags, remember?

My favorite rejection letter was from a New York agent who said, "We don't have time to take any more clients and if we did, we wouldn't take you."

Thanks.

No, really.

He helped me brew my tea.

I started writing fiction because I wanted to see in books the kind of women I saw in real life. I grew up with a strong, funny, and feisty mom; Mother Mary, whom you will meet herein. She taught me the dangers of swimming too soon after you eat, and also that toasters are out to electrocute you. She ran our family, The Flying Scottolines, alternating kisses and hugs with swats from a wooden spoon. Her tomato sauce was the glue that held us together, and her kitchen table was more powerful than a conference table in any Fortune 500 company.

But when I read popular novels, I didn't see any women like my mother, my girl-friends, or even myself. The women were all minor characters — wives, girlfriends, and/or hookers — and their characterization was as thin as a thong.

In short, women never got to star in books, and it got me wondering. How are we supposed to star in our own lives, if we never see that anywhere around us? How can our daughters realize their fullest potential, if they're still pouring coffee in fiction?

So I started to write stories starring ordinary women, who are extraordinary in so many ways. I'm talking about teachers, lawyers, journalists, at-home moms, judges, dentists, and nurses.

In short, tea bags.

My characters get themselves into hot water and out again, stronger and better for it. Just like life. Sixteen years and sixteen books later, the books are bestsellers, thanks to you.

(Big hug.)

My trademark heroine is everything I want to be, or how I feel on a good hair day. Interviewers always ask me if I'll write a novel with a male as the main character, (a question no male author is ever asked), and here is what I answer:

"No."

"Why?" they ask.

"Because I have ovaries. And I write what I know."

It was so good to be writing books about extraordinary ordinary women, I thought it would be even better if I wrote about them for the newspaper, too, so I started a weekly column called "Chick Wit" for *The Philadelphia Inquirer.* Now I've rewritten those columns, added some new ones, and turned them into this little book.

In the next pages, you'll read about the amazing adventures of our everyday lives — like wrestling with Spanx, juggling hockey and soccer practices, and trying to keep our roots touched up. I also offer plenty of useful advice, like how to survive Valentine's Day, why you should embrace visible panty lines, and that you should throw away your iron, immediately. The stories that follow are in no particular order, and together they're a mix tape for moms and girls.

In short, tea bags.

As for the cast of characters, you'll meet my real-life family, starting with Mother Mary, she of the traveling back scratcher. And Brother Frank, who's gay and lives in Miami with Mother Mary, in a small house that smells of ravioli and really strong aftershave. There's daughter Francesca, now a budding author who writes herein to give her generation's take on things. And finally beloved father Frank, who has passed on, except for his soul, which guides me in life and also on 1-95.

There's also best friend Franca and assistant Laura, who are so alike that they're

10

almost the same extraordinary woman, but in different bodies. Every girl needs girlfriends, and they are my besties. If I killed somebody, they would show up with shovels and Hefty bags. A girlfriend is just another word for accessory after the fact.

And you'll also meet the disobedient pets that fill my life, and unfortunately, my bed. As of this writing, I have four dogs on rotation — two golden retrievers, a corgi, and a newest addition, Little Tony The Anatomically Incorrect Puppy. I also support two cats, a flock of chickens, and an ancient 4-H pony, Buddy. Whoever says you can't buy love has never had a pet.

Finally, appearing in these pages are my two ex-husbands, Thing One and Thing Two. They are minor characters.

Bottom line, I'm a woman on my own. I'm betting you can relate, even if you're married or sharing your bed with something other than a golden retriever. In the end, we are all of us on our own.

And that's good news.

Because we're strong enough to star in our own lives.

And we tea bags make a helluva cup of tea.

I hope you enjoy this book. I think it's funny, emotional, and true. You'll laugh,

you'll cry, and you'll swear off panty-hose.
Welcome to my world.
And yours, too.
Tea bags, unite!
Let's start a revolution.

A woman is like a tea bag. You never know how strong she is until she's in hot water.
— Eleanor Roosevelt

OF DOGS AND MEN

I'm old enough to remember Ozzie and Harriet, which means that my idea of the nuclear family was born in the 1950s and never quite grew up. By that I mean, a family has a Mommy, a Daddy, and two kids. And a dog.

Run, Spot, run!

We all know that the nuclear family has changed, but what's interesting to me is that nobody has just one dog anymore.

I'm not sure when it started, but all of the people who used to have a family dog now have family dogs. I myself have a full herd — three golden retrievers and one Pembroke Welsh corgi, who rules us all. Multiple dogs used to be thought of as crazy. Fifteen years ago, when I used to walk two dogs in the city, people asked me if both dogs were mine. Now I walk four and nobody raises an eyebrow.

This is true on TV as well. More and

more, we see two dogs chowing down in Iams commercials, side-by-side. The Dog Whisperer, Cesar Milan, spends many of his episodes trying to get all of us crazies with multiple dogs to live happily together.

So when exactly did people start acquiring multiple dogs?

And why?

Before you answer, consider another phenomenon, which I sense is related. What caused the nuclear family to blow up was that people started getting divorced like crazy. All of a sudden, the divorces began to pile up. I don't mean across-the-country, I mean in one person. People I met had acquired second and third divorces almost as easily as they had acquired second and third dogs. At some point, the third divorce became the new second divorce. No one even bothered to count their first divorce. People didn't tell their third set of kids about it. It happened so long ago, you could easily forget.

Nowadays, even normal people are on their second divorce. People like me, for example. I have two ex-husbands, Thing One and Thing Two. To be honest, I used to be embarrassed about being divorced twice. When people asked me if I was married, I would simply answer, "No, I'm divorced."

Okay, technically it was the truth, but lawyers would call it a material omission. Sooner or later, my pathetic personal history would spill out, and I'd be busted.

But recently, I was speaking at a library in California, and I met a lot of very nice women my age. And when I mumbled something about being divorced twice, one of them said, "Don't worry about it, honey, I'm divorced four times." And somebody else chirped up, "I'm on my third." And another chimed in, "I'm on my fifth!"

Boy, did that make me feel great! Er, I mean, it made me feel terribly concerned for the future of our nation and the American family.

And the funny thing is, many of these women had multiple dogs. Everyone I spoke with who had more than one dog also had more than one divorce. Some women had more divorces than dogs, others had more dogs than divorces. It makes you wonder which came first — the dog or the divorce?

Is the new dog acquired as a result of the new divorce? In other words, do we trade our husband in for a dog?

Or does getting yet another Yorkie lead to your fourth divorce?

Are we replacing stable human families with stable dog families?

You may think I'm comparing two unrelated things, but this really isn't so crazy when you consider that many women, myself included, sleep with their dogs on the bed. In fact, in my own case, three of my dogs sleep on what used to be my ex's side of the bed. Plus, dogs do a lot of the things husbands do; snore, toss and turn, and fart. And I think my corgi has restless leg syndrome.

I believe these things are related. From my side of the bed, I'm smelling a connection.

The only thing that's missing is the prenup.

BODY PARTS

I like to write about the differences between men and women, but this time I thought I'd bring up something we have in common. Namely, that we can't always control our eyes.

For a long time now, men have gotten a lot of grief when they look at a woman's chest instead of her eyes. Mostly everybody has made that observation, so that men are terrified to look anywhere but directly into our eyes. It's gotten to the point that if a weird bony hand burst through a woman's sternum, like in the movie *Alien,* the man she was talking to would be the last to notice. Or if he knew, he'd be too afraid to admit it, lest he incur the wrath of Sigourney Weaver.

It's not really fair to men.

First of all, it's only natural for a man to wonder what a woman's chest looks like. Men have testosterone for a reason, and if they don't use it up looking at our chests, then they'll be causing wars and football playoffs.

Second, women are getting boob jobs left and right, so to speak. It's a mixed message to spend all that money on a new and improved chest, then get angry when a man notices your purchase. Women can't have it both ways.

Third, what's happening now is that a man will spend so much time staring fixedly into a woman's eyes that she'll wonder if her eye makeup is sliding off or if he has a David Copperfield thing and is trying to mesmerize her. Hyp-mo-tized!

It's tough to be a man, with eyes, when breasts are around.

And women are having their own eye issues lately. There's a male body part I always check out before I look at a man's face. And frankly, if this body part doesn't pass the test, I never get to his face. In fact, if this body part doesn't go my way, I don't even care if he has a face.

I'm talking about the ring finger.

It's gotten to be a very bad habit with me. It's not like I'm on the prowl, or that I want to get married again, because I don't. My Future Ex-Husband will be very carefully chosen, because after Strike Two, well, you know. Still I find myself checking out ring fingers to see if a man is married, everywhere I go. At Staples. At a party. Even driving on the turnpike.

In fact, I'm pretty sure that if a man killed somebody in front of me and the police called me as an eyewitness, I couldn't describe him at all if he had a wedding band on. Married men can get away with murder when I'm around.

I could give a detailed description of their ring, however.

Even weirder, I check out ring fingers as if there's a doubt about the outcome, which there isn't. Every man I see is married. Every man I know is married. Every man I don't see and don't know is married. Checking ring fingers is like watching *The Godfather* over and over, and hoping Don Corleone doesn't die in the tomato patch.

And then the other day I found myself in the awful predicament that men must get into when they're talking to a woman they're attracted to and they want to check out her chest, but they can't because the woman is watching their eyes to see where they go. I happened to be talking to this attractive man, having a conversation that was unusually entertaining, or at least not about his wife or kids for a change, when I realized

21

that by some stroke of temporary insanity, I had forgotten to check out his ring finger first.

Arg!

Then he kept talking and being more charming and getting handsomer by the minute, and I kept wondering, is he married or not? I kept waiting for the right moment to sneak a peek at his ring finger, but I knew he would see my eyes look down because he was staring so fixedly into my pupils, because he wasn't allowed to sneak a peek at my chest. I knew I wasn't supposed to reduce him to a finger anymore than he was supposed to reduce me to a chest, and for a time, we were almost in danger of getting to know one another.

What a waste of time!

But luckily, our eyes got teary from all that staring, and we both lost interest in the conversation because we couldn't get the answer we really wanted.

So what happened?

He turned away first, and I got my answer. Married. So I wasn't interested.

Then he got his answer. 34 A. So he wasn't interested.

And don't get me started on married men who don't wear wedding rings.

Busted!

Everything Old Is Nude Again

Something dangerous is going on in the world of women's underwear, and I want to nip it in the butt.

Sorry.

I am referring, of course, to Spanx.

If you don't know what Spanx are, I have one word for you:

Girdles.

I got introduced to Spanx by accident, when I bought a black-patterned pair, thinking they were tights. I got my size, which is B.

For Beautiful.

I took them home and put them on, which was like slipping into a tourniquet. Then I realized they weren't tights, they were just Tight, and I checked the box, which read Tight-End Tights.

Huh?

I actually managed to squeeze myself into them, then I put on a knit dress, examined myself in the mirror, and hated what I saw. From the front, I looked like a Tootsie Roll with legs. From the back, instead of having buttocks, I had buttock.

In other words, my lower body had been transformed into a cylinder. I no longer had hips where hips are supposed to be, or saddlebags where God intended. I was the cardboard in the roll of toilet paper.

And another detail. I couldn't breathe.

Also the elastic waistband was giving me a do-it-yourself hysterectomy.

I didn't understand the product, so I went instantly to the website, which explained that these were no ordinary tights but were "slimming apparel." This, under the bright pink banner that read, "It's what's on the inside that counts!"

Really?

The website claimed that "these innovative undergarments eliminate VBL (visible bra lines) and VPL (visible panty lines)."

Well.

Would this be a good time to say that I'm in favor of VBL and VPL? Especially VPL. In fact, I want my P as V as possible.

You know why?

Because I wear P.

I don't know what kind of signal we're sending if we want our butts to suggest otherwise. Bottom line, I'm not the kind of girl who goes without P. In other words, I'm a Good Girl (GG). And GGs wear P.

Same goes for B.

I admit, I get a little lazy, especially at home or in the emergency room, as you will learn later. I don't always bother with B all the time. But if I'm in public and not wearing a down coat, I wear B. And I also want my B to be V.

You know why?

I want extra credit.

If I went to the trouble to put on a B, I want to be recognized for it. Here's an analogy; I'm not the kind of person who makes charitable donations anonymously. If I give away money, I want a plaque or maybe a stadium named after me, so everybody knows that I'm nice, in addition to being good. (N and G). In fact, that makes me a N and GG.

But back to P and B.

I went back to the mirror and noticed something else — that the fat that properly belonged on my hips, having taken up residence there at age 40, was now homeless and being relocated upward by my tights, leaving a roll at my waist which could pass for a flotation device.

But have no fear. I checked the website,

and Spanx has the solution: "slimming camis." That is, camisoles that look like Ace bandages, which presumably pick up the fat roll at the waist and squeeze it upward, so that, having nowhere else to go, it pops out on top, as breasts.

Ta-da!

Or rather, ta-tas!

This is interesting, for physics. Natural law says that matter cannot be created or destroyed, but that was pre-Spanx. With these babies, you could destroy the matter at your waistline and increase it at your bustline, merely by turning your body into a half-squeezed tube of toothpaste.

And of course, you'll need a new bra to catch all your homeless fat, so the website sells "the Bra-llelujah!" It even states, "So, say goodbye to BBS (Bad Bra Syndrome)!"

Thank God. I hate it when my B is B.

I looked at the other articles of slimming apparel, and there were even tights for pregnant women, which was great. I wouldn't want my baby to be born with VIL (Visible Infant Lines).

And there were Power Panties, which made me smile.

If women had power, we wouldn't need Spanx.

DEFEATED

I was driving down the street the other day when I saw a sign on an empty storefront that read, FISH PEDICURES COMING SOON!

It was the kind of sign that got me thinking. Do fish need pedicures? You'd think they would do without, in this economy.

Unless they were goldfish.

I went home and plugged "fish pedicures" into Google, and I learned that this is a new kind of pedicure for women, whereby you plunge your feet into a tank of water and fish eat your dead skin off.

I'm not joking.

The article said that fish pedicures use doctor fish, who evidently love this sort of thing. You have to wonder why they didn't put their medical degree to better use. To me, the only thing more disgusting than putting your feet in a bucket of flesh-eating fish is being a fish who has to eat dead skin for dinner.

Yuck.

I don't have time to get pedicures, though I love them. The last one I had, my feet came out clean and smooth as a saint's, except for the red nail polish. I opted for red because if you're going to get a pedicure once a year, you have to make it count. Red toenail polish signals that you're single and ready to mingle, at least in your mind.

Otherwise, the sight of a middle-aged woman's foot is not for the fainthearted, especially in mid-winter. Only women have the constitution to deal with it, like childbirth and diaper genies.

I can barely stomach trimming my own toenails, which I do with one of those cheapo stainless-steel clippers from CVS. I try to cut them evenly, but they always end up pointy enough to qualify as a lethal weapon in most jurisdictions.

Plus, my scientific observation is that nails thicken with time, so that a fifty-year-old toenail has the thickness of a ram's horn and is almost as pretty. My toenail trimming would go a lot faster if I replaced the clipper with a chainsaw.

And then there are calluses, which are fun. I can't imagine a doctor fish eating through my calluses, unless he was a surgeon fish.

Or a sturgeon fish.

Plus my calluses have toughened as the years have gone by, adding layer after layer, like the Earth's crust. Sometimes the calluses sprout cracks like fault lines, and when they finally split open, I have my own personal earthquake.

My feet are a natural disaster.

Daughter Francesca is grossed out by my feet, but they have their advantages. I don't have to wear shoes, as I appear to be growing my own pair of wooden clogs.

I don't need a pedicurist, I need a blacksmith.

Of course, my toes are no picnic, either. I don't know when this happened, maybe at about age 40, but all my toes have been become one. In other words, where I used have five vertical toes on each foot, I now appear to have one toe on each foot, but it's horizontal.

Please tell me this happened to you, too.

And what's up with our little toe?

Do you even have a little toe anymore? What happens to that little toe, when we get older? Has it been ignored for so long that it simply decides to vanish? Does it say to itself, I wonder if anybody will even notice that I'm gone?

If you ask me, that little piggy is going to market and never coming back.

The saddest thing about the little toe is the littlest toenail.

Can you even see yours, ladies?

I don't know if you have the Amazing Disappearing Toenail, but I do. About 10 years ago, it was normal size, then it magically cut itself in half, then in half again and again. Now it's a toe sliver. If I could lose weight like my littlest toenail, I'd be Lindsay Lohan.

Bottom line, the fish pedicure isn't for me. Even a shark would throw up his hands.

CLASSIFIED PORN

Everybody has their pornography, and mine is the real estate ads. I don't know when this happened or why, but I read the real estate ads with the absorption of a pervert.

At the outset, I should make it clear that I love my house. I have no intention of moving, ever. But I still can't wait to get the Sunday paper and start house-shopping.

I gaze lovingly at ads for condos in town and new construction in far suburbs. I look at duplexes and ranchers, Cape Cods and mansions. I look at houses that are way too expensive as well as ones that aren't half as nice as my house. I study the photos of the Featured Properties and wonder if the stone front is only a façade or goes all the way around. Is that front lawn as big as it looks?

It might be cool to live in a Featured Property instead of a normal house, presumably featureless.

And then there's the ad copy, which can't

be deciphered without a decoder ring. What is a "Custm/grmt/KIT/isl/Cor"? I translate "custom kitchen with a Corian island" because I'm a professional. But the "grmt" stumps me. A misprint for granite? And what about a "new LL rec rm/wine clr?" I understand a new recreation room with a wine cellar, but what's LL?

It's a mystery, delicious and tantalizing, which only enhances the sensuality of the ads. It's real estate, semi-nude.

I flip to the shore properties and read about the beach houses. It would be nice to have a beach house, wouldn't it? I love the beach. Lots of people have second houses, why shouldn't I? Today there's a SOLD stamp over the photo of a four-bedroom at the Jersey shore, and the sight fills me with dismay. Now I couldn't buy the beach house even if I wanted to.

Which I didn't.

This is what I think about as I scan the ads for homes that I will never buy. It's like daydreaming about how I'd spend Powerball winnings though I never play the lottery, which is another of my fantasies.

I know that none of this makes any sense. When I finally bought my house, I was so glad that I wouldn't have to read the Sunday paper anymore and go house-shopping. But that was years ago, and I'm still house-shopping.

Why?

And before you answer, I should disclose that I do the same thing with the pet ads. I read all the dog ads, each one, even for bull mastiffs, Rottweiler, Boston Terriers, and Boxers. I check out the new breeds like goldendoodles and maltipoos. I imagine these little furballs as I skim one ad after the other.

Of course, I'm not in the market for a new dog, much less a bull mastiff. I have four dogs, yet I compare prices of shihpoos, whatever that is.

I love the doggie ad copy, too. Special Little Friends. Cute N' Cuddly. Precious Little Bed Bugs. The one line that always gets me is Needs Good Home. If a puppy Needs Good Home, I consider buying whatever breed they're selling. I can't take the guilt.

I have Good Home, even though I could have Better Home, according to the real estate ads.

If I had Featured Property, I'd buy two puppies.

What is the matter with me? Why do I do this, and am I the only one?

Before you render your diagnosis, you should have all the facts. I don't read the classified ads for jobs or cars. This might lead you to conclude that I'm more satisfied with my job and car than with my house and pets. But that's not true.

I like my job and car just fine, but not more than everything else. In fact, if I were to list my Top Ten Necessities, they would be:

1. family
2. dogs
3. house
4. job
5. car
6. Starbucks vente iced green-tea latte, breve, no melon syrup, light ice
7. Caesar salad, dressing on the side, no croutons
8. strawberry preserves
9. Splenda
10. oxygen

So, clearly I'm looking at the ads of things I love the most. I guess it's so I can dream about more of a great thing. Or maybe it's because I'm a woman.

I wonder if men read car ads for porn the way women read real estate ads.

My guess is, are you kidding?

EARTHQUAKE MARY

I am a mother, I have a mother, and I love mothers. I think mothers are a natural force, and maybe an alternative source of fuel.

Observe.

My mother, Mother Mary, lives with brother Frank in South Beach. She awoke one morning with a start, convinced that her bed had moved during sleep, as if there had been an earthquake. But nothing was out of place in her bedroom, and it was a cloudless Sunday, still as a postcard. Nevertheless, she was sure there had been an earthquake. She went and woke up my brother, who told her to go back to sleep.

She didn't. She scurried across the street like an octogenarian Chicken Little, to warn their neighbor. He told her to go back to sleep, too.

Instead she went home and called the *Miami Herald.*

She told the reporter about the earthquake, and he told her that the sky wasn't falling and suggested she go back to sleep. He also took her name and telephone number, which turned out to be a good thing, because he had to call her back, later that day.

She had been absolutely right. There had been an earthquake, at the exact time she had felt it.

The clincher? The earthquake occurred 397 miles from Miami, in Tampa. And the only person who felt it in Miami was my mother, Mary Scottoline.

I'm not kidding.

Soon, TV newsvans began arriving at my mother's house. My brother, who you may remember is gay, told me he put on his "best tank top."

The Scottolines have style.

The reporters interviewed my mother, and under her picture on the TV screen, the banner read EARTHQUAKE MARY. They asked her how she felt an earthquake that took place so far away. She answered that she "knows about these things."

The MIAMI HERALD published the story, as reported by Martin Merzer and Aldo Nahed. My favorite part reads, "It was a pretty nice weekend in Florida. Except, you know, for the 6.0 magnitude earthquake . . . In

South Florida, the event passed virtually unnoticed, though Mary Scottoline, 82 . . ."

If you don't believe me, go and find the story online. Google "Mary Scottoline." Or "I-Told-You-I'm-Not-Crazy Scottoline," "Nobody-Ever-Listens-To Me-Scottoline," or "You-And-Your Brother-Think-You-Know-Everything-with-that-Cockamamie-Computer Scottoline."

It wasn't the first time that Mother Mary had something in common with a natural disaster. Once I made her fly north to me to avoid a hurricane, and she wasn't happy about it. When she got off the plane, a TV reporter stuck a microphone in her face and asked if she was afraid of the hurricane. She answered:

"I'm not afraid of a hurricane. I *am* a hurricane."

So you see what we're dealing with. A force of nature. A four-foot-eleven bundle of heart, bile, and moxie.

And superpowers.

I've known for a long time that Mother Mary has superpowers. She used to cast off the evil eye when somebody gave me a "whammy," by chanting a secret spell over a bowl of water and olive oil. She dipped her fingers in the water, made the sign of the cross on my forehead, and whispered mysterious words that sounded like *osso bucco.* This spell was handed down to her by another Italian Mother/Witch on Christmas Eve, which is the only time it can be told. She won't tell me the spell because I'm a lawyer.

But I digress.

Your mother may not smear olive oil on your face, but she has superpowers, too. Spider-Man has nothing on mothers.

We don't think of mothers as having superpowers, but they do. Mothers can tell what we're doing when their backs are turned to us. They know we have a fever without a thermometer. They can be at three places at once, a soccer game, a violin lesson, and the high school play, even if it's *Annie.* They can tell we're sad by the way we say, "I'm fine."

And, magically, they can change us into them, without us even knowing how or when. Mother Mary used to make me call her when I got home and let the phone ring three times, as a signal. (This, in a time when long distance calls cost money.) I thought it was silly, but she said, "When you're a mother, you'll understand."

And finally, I do.

TOPLESS

You know how they tell you to wear clean underwear in case you're in an accident? Well, this story is almost like that.

Until Sunday night, my weekend was terrific. I went to New York for an opera marathon; Friday night was *Madama Butterfly*, Saturday matinee *Le Nozze di Figaro*, and Saturday night, *Lucia di Lammermoor*. Bottom line, for most of my waking hours, people were singing to me.

And if that's not great enough, chocolate was involved.

Opera candy isn't as good as movie candy, in that there are no Raisinets, but at least they have vaguely European chocolate bars that taste pretentious. I made do with the dark chocolate for the nighttime shows and switched to milk chocolate for the matinee, but in any event, as you can tell from the opera and the chocolate, I tend to overdo things. Which is why I have four dogs, but

I'm getting ahead of myself.

So I came home and on Sunday night was having a wonderful time poring over my Playbills when a fight broke out between my old golden retriever Lucy and Ruby The Corgi. I leaped into action to break it up, stuck my index finger into the canines of some canine, and got bitten. Not to be a diva about it, but this was no little baby puncture wound. When I looked down at my finger, it no longer had a top.

And there was blood. Not as much as Lucia di Lammermoor, but enough to send Madame Butterfly running for her car keys and flying to the hospital. I hustled into the emergency room with one hand held high, which was when I remembered something:

I was braless.

Kind reader, my adventures can get personal from time to time. It's never been quite this personal, but I think it's important to deal with this subject, to be sure you girls out there learn from my mistake.

Here's my lesson: you have to wear your bra all the time, even in the house when you're relaxing by yourself after a busy weekend eating chocolate to music. Because you never know if something untoward is going to happen and you're going to find yourself in a hospital emergency room in no bra.

At the same time that you're middle-aged.

The first clue that I had forgotten my underwear was the running part. Yes, that's it, running into the emergency room with my hand up in the air. The second clue was the look on the face of the hot male nurse when he came into the room to examine my finger. Because, of course, on the night that your dog bites your finger, the nurse will be male and hot. (Lately, I'm thinking that men divide into two groups: Married or Learner's Permit. The nurse was the latter, which is more entertaining, if equally off limits.)

Anyway, I could tell from his look that I'd crossed the line.

You know which line I mean. The Point of No Return, Bralessness-wise.

When I was younger, going braless was fun and sexy. I wasn't above resorting to bralessness, as needed. It was one of my female bag of tricks. The other was whining. Men love that.

The point is that bralessness used to work. But that was then, and this is now.

Now, I wouldn't be caught in public without a bra. Now, I buy costly bras that not only lift and separate, but also hoist, buttress, cantilever, and generally defy gravity and other natural laws. Isaac Newton had nothing on my underwear.

Einstein's Theory is no match for Victoria's Secret.

In my younger days, I scorned padded bras. Now I demand them. Although now they're called "formed," which costs twenty dollars more than padded, but we both know what we're talking about:

Extra credit.

A little help.

False advertising.

Except that here I was sitting in front of a hot male nurse, and I was wearing crappy jeans and a sweater that wasn't slouchy enough. Truth to tell, no sweater is slouchy enough for my breasts, unimproved. The nurse gallantly averted his eyes, or maybe he was just nauseated. To his credit, he tried to stop the blood flowing from my finger and made small talk to distract me from the horror of the situation and also the fact that my finger was bloody.

He asked me, "Why do you have four dogs?"

"That's just how I roll. And don't get me started on opera and chocolate." Silence followed, so I asked, "What do you think happened to the top of my finger? I didn't see it on the floor."

"Your dog probably ate it. They're carnivores, you know."

Yuck. I couldn't speak for a moment. That my dog bit my finger is one thing. That my dog ate my finger is quite another. Not only was I grossed out, I wondered how I would be able to write. I type with two index fingers, and only one was open for business. Then I considered the bright side. If I missed my deadline, I wouldn't have to say to my editor, My dog ate my homework. I had a much better excuse: My dog ate *me*.

But the nurse was shaking his head. "Looks like you need a skin graft. Tomorrow, you'll have to see a hand surgeon."

"Thanks," I said, but this is what I thought:

Now *that* calls for an underwire.

GETTING RELIGION

I understand that there's a religion that allows polygamy, so that a man can have as many wives as he pleases. To be fair, I'm not sure this is exactly the religion, but it's the religion on the TV show, so it may only be an HBO-sanctioned religion.

But that's not my point.

My point is, where is the religion that allows a woman to have as many husbands as she pleases?

I could get very religious about a religion like that, but there isn't one. It's like *The Stepford Wives,* where the wives are robots who do everything to please their husbands. What I want to know is, where are the Stepford Husbands?

You know why it's set up this way. The book that started the religion was written by a man, and the book that started the Stepford Wives was written by a man.

Well, I write books, too. Can I start a

44

religion?

In my religion, wives could have as many husbands as they wanted. So far, I've had as many ex-husbands as I wanted, but that's not the same thing.

You can see how my new religion would open up a world of possibilities. For example, in my life, neither Thing One nor Thing Two was very handy around the house. So my first new husband would have to be handy. I'll call him Fix-it Hubby. I really like a guy who can fix the doorbell. Or that rubber thing inside the toilet tank that's supposed to flop up and down. Things have gotten so bad around my house that, last week, a friend of mine sent her husband over to fix that rubber thing.

That was when I turned to religion to solve my problems.

My second new husband would have to be sexy, and if you need me to tell you what he's for, you're new around here. I'll call him Sexy Hubby. Every woman has her own idea about what constitutes sexy, but mine involves chest hair.

My third new husband would do chores, like take out the trash and unload the groceries. Chores are all I'd ever ask of this very lucky man. I hate to do chores, and who doesn't? I'll call him Chore Hubby.

And my fourth new husband would have to be a great cook. It would be fun to have a husband who cooks, especially if he looks like Chef Tom Colicchio on *Top Chef.*

I'll call him Tom Colicchio.

How great is this religion, so far?

I think women would love this religion, and so would men. The advantages for women are obvious, but there are plenty of advantages for men, too. After all, it means that your husbands could avoid the more tiresome of your marital duties. For example, you could be Sexy Hubby and leave fixing the toilet to Toilet Hubby.

Or vice versa, if it's playoff season. You only have to fix a toilet once and it stays fixed, if you follow.

My new religion is also good for men, because, frankly, I know a lot of women who are a Handful. Actually, I've figured out that I'm a Handful. So of course, any woman worth having is a Handful. But in my religion, all the hubbies could band together to keep the Handful happy, and that creates certain efficiencies and economies of scale, which is the kind of thing men love.

Because it leaves more time for the playoffs.

The other great thing about my new religion is that there would never be divorce.

If you got sick of Toilet Hubby, you wouldn't have to divorce him, you could just marry Car Inspection Hubby. It's really annoying to have to get the car inspected all the time, and you can never find your registration card. In fact, you could marry Registration Hubby, too. And Proof-of-Insurance Hubby.

Why not?

Then you wouldn't ever have to leave the bedroom.

If you follow.

Finally, the best thing about my religion would be who got worshipped. In the religion where you have tons of wives, they all worship the husband. And if you have lots of robot wives, they worship the husbands, too.

So you see where this is going.

Wanna join?

Have It My Way

I used to think of myself as low-maintenance. I used to believe I was easy to please. But now I know better.

Starbucks taught me the truth.

My order at Starbucks is a vente iced green-tea latte, breve, no melon syrup, light ice. I love my drink. It's a treat I give myself a few times a week. I give myself all manner of food rewards, because I'm an emotional eater. Can you think of a better reason to eat?

But back to Starbucks. I was standing in line behind a tall sugar-free cinnamon dolce latte with nonfat milk no-whip, who was standing behind a grande iced non-fat no-whip mocha. When it came to my turn, I gave my order and watched my hard-working barista like a disapproving mother, to make sure he didn't add the melon syrup.

One time, my barista made a mistake and added the melon syrup. I took a sip and then threw the entire drink away. I won't drink it with the melon syrup. And I couldn't bring myself to ask the barista to redo it, because I couldn't admit to him or myself that I'd become a woman who refuses to drink something that isn't exactly the way she wants it.

But I have.

I always order salads with the dressing on the side and no croutons. I always use Splenda and not Equal. I like Half-and-Half or light cream in my coffee, but not milk. I like strawberry preserves, but don't come near with me with strawberry jelly.

How did I get like this?

I was standing in Whole Foods the other day, mesmerized by the yogurt. I used to be fine with normal vanilla yogurt, then I switched to strawberry. But here I was, dazzled in the dairy aisle, astounded by white yogurt containers gleaming like pearls on a strand. There was normal yogurt from cows, but there was also goat's milk yogurt, buffalo milk yogurt, nonfat yogurt, low-fat yogurt, and yogurt in a bottle, so you could drink it. There was yogurt with normal bacteria and yogurt with special bacteria.

Uh-oh. I had no idea how to choose bacteria. Generally, bacteria is the kind of thing I like to avoid.

In short, I could have it the way I wanted, but I wasn't sure how I wanted it. Then I started to wonder about when all these choices began, and when we started to customize germs.

Maybe it goes back to Burger King's "Have it Your Way" campaign. Before then, back when we didn't know better, we ate hamburgers with whatever they put on them. The Burger King campaign was a response to McDonald's "Have it Our Way" approach, which meant that every burger came with a pickle, ketchup, and chopped onion bits.

In those days, if you didn't like the pickle, you were forced to take matters into your own hands. You had to handle the situation all by yourself. You had to take the pickle off.

Likewise, if you didn't like ketchup, you had to cope. You either had to eat your hamburger with the ketchup and try to live another day, or you had to find yourself a plastic knife and scrape that ketchup right off.

We were like MacGyver then, full of ingenuity.

But those days are over. We started having it our way and we never stopped. And somewhere along the line, there sprung up

300 million choices for every product, and I became the pickiest person on the planet.

That's it. It must be Burger King's fault. Because it can't be mine.

But here's the hard question: Have all these choices made us happier? Am I really, truly, happier for all of those choices?

Absolutely.

I love it. I love having everything exactly the way I want it. I work hard to earn the money to buy myself my food rewards. I'm like a puppy giving myself Milk Bones — which come in cheese, liver, and regular flavor.

And I even love the dairy aisle, dazzling me with choice. When I clap eyes on all those yogurts, my heart swells with pride. I'm lucky to live in a country armed with powerful marketing weapons, all of which are aimed at little old me. They've succeeded in convincing me that there really is a difference between these products, and that the difference is critical.

And so I choose.

In fact, I'm going to start sampling soon, and in a week or so, I'll have selected my absolute favorite bacteria.

I hope it comes in hazelnut.

Movie Time

Recently, I went to the movies and saw one of the worst movies ever. But I had a great time, for one reason:

Movie candy.

I used to think that I loved the movies, but I realized what I love is movie candy.

What's so great about movie candy is that I allow myself to have it at all. I'm in carb rehab, so I'd never eat popcorn at home. Nor would I ever eat candy, normally. But at a movie, I'm allowed to get popcorn and candy, both. In fact, I'm entitled. A movie theater is Switzerland of the diet world.

The same goes for portion control. I'm careful about my portions, but not at the movies. All movie candy has one portion size. Two hours.

Movie popcorn isn't food, it's gambling. You never know if you'll win or lose. Most often, you lose, because movie popcorn can taste like blown-in fiberglass insulation or paper, salted. Sometimes you win, and get a bag like I had the other night — a lovely canary gold, freshly popped, tasting of real Jersey corn. That's one win in forty-odd years of movie popcorn. Yet, gambler that I am, I know that I'll hit the jackpot again someday. That's why I keep playing movie popcorn.

In contrast, the appeal of movie candy is its very predictability. If movie popcorn is a date, movie candy is a marriage. It always tastes the same, so much so that you can have a certain go-to movie candy for years. Raisinets has been my favorite movie candy for the past decade. It never disappoints. It always tastes chewy, soft, chocolaty, and vaguely healthy. My relationship to Raisinets has lasted longer than both my marriages, and cost me far less.

Before Raisinets, for me there was only Goobers, again for almost ten years. It wasn't cheating to switch from Goobers to Raisinets, because both are in the same movie candy food group, namely Chocolate Contaminated by Natural Foods.

The decade before that, I always went with Whoppers, which were from a related food group, Chocolate Contaminated by Unnatural Foods.

I used to love Whoppers, chocolate-covered malted milk balls that come in a faux milk carton, a reminder of their faux-dairy origins. I stopped eating Whoppers only when I kept encountering what daughter Francesca calls the Dead Whopper.

The Dead Whopper looks alive on the outside — smooth, round, shiny, and almost brown. But as soon as you bite down, you know. The Dead Whopper collapses instead of crunching, and flattens to a gummy rock. It doesn't taste like chocolate, it just tastes brown. And there you are, stuck with a cheekful of Dead Whopper and no napkin. It takes trust to eat candy in pitch darkness, and the Dead Whopper breaks its vows.

So I divorced Whoppers. I aim for quality control in my candy marriages.

Back in my youth, my movie candy came only from the High Maintenance Group, composed of Jujyfruits, Dots, and the immortal Jujubes. This group contains fruit plastic pressed into unrecognizable shapes and tinted the color of unpopular crayons. I used to love candy from this group because I was younger and had more time to deal with their candy drama.

The High Maintenance Group required a do-it-yourself dental scaling, right there in the movie seat, with your fingernail. It was labor intensive, not to mention disgusting. Picking your teeth and eating what you retrieve is acceptable only for eight-year-olds and under.

The High Maintenance Group also required you to hold the candy up to the movie screen to determine its color/flavor. I can't tell you how many movies I saw through a Lysol-yellow Jujyfruits filter. I liked only the red and black Jujyfruits, so I had to perform the ritual of finding them by the light of the screen, then dumping the orange, green, and yellows back into the box. In no time, only the colors I hated were left, so I had to rank them, then eat them in descending order of hate.

It required a lot of decision-making, for a candy.

No candy was more high maintenance than Jujubes, the founding candy of the group. I think they may be defunct now, because I never see Jujubes at the movies anymore. I admired Jujubes for their moxie, not to mention their enigmatic name. They weren't people-pleasers, like Raisinets. Jujubes dared you to like them. They made too much noise, as if they wanted out of their narrow box. They could crack a molar. Their colors were profoundly ugly. They tasted like drill bits.

And you know what?
I miss them.

There is underrated. There is a sleeper. There doesn't get much hype, but there is about love and devotion. About constancy and sacrifice.

Here is my wish for you:

On Father's Day, may you be lucky enough to have your father there.

BABY BIRD

I am a woman who likes routines, but now that daughter Francesca is home from college for the summer, the times they are a-changing.

By way of background, she is my only child and I'm a single parent, so it's just the two of us. Even so, I had gotten used to the empty-nest thing. I liked everything being in order, or at least in my favorite form of disarray. I had my own hours and habits. I walked in the morning with the dogs. Worked all day. Cooked something simple and light during the evening news. Worked at night or read, guilt-free. Showered as necessary.

But my baby bird is back, and she's wrenched my life out of shape. For example, I had to move all of my winter clothes, boxes, and books out of her room, as she insisted on having a bed.

Annoying.

Also, she thought it would be fun if we got a kitten, and I went along. But somehow we couldn't leave with only one kitten, so we got two. When we took them home, I learned that one plus one doesn't equal two, when it comes to kittens. Looking at my house now, you would think I hired a kitten wrecking crew. Their names are Mimi and Vivi, and they're conspiring as we speak. They shred toilet paper. They climb table lamps. They surf throw pillows. By the way, we already had four pets — three golden retrievers and a bossy Welsh corgi — and you can imagine their happiness at the new arrivals. The goldens think the kittens are delicious. The corgi thinks she gave birth.

My schedule is a mess, too. Francesca's become a vegetarian, so we go food-shopping all the time. We're in the market, squinting at labels and scanning for magic words like cruelty-free. What's the alternative? Pro-cruelty? Obviously she's right, but all of a sudden, I'm spending too much of my life around produce. Plus, I'm carb-free, which means that we agree only on celery.

I don't recognize my own shopping cart. I buy Bocaburgers and tempeh like they're going out of style. This is food you couldn't pick out of a lineup. Bocaburgers look like coasters, and tempeh looks like fiberglass.

I've eaten Bocaburgers, so I know they're good with ketchup, because everything is good with ketchup. As for tempeh, I have no idea what it tastes like or how to prepare it. I'm thinking sautéed. With ketchup.

Worse yet, Francesca likes clean clothes, which I regard as picky. Living alone, I have gone months without doing laundry. I work at home, and the UPS man doesn't care if I wear the same T-shirt and shorts all week. So does he.

But now dirty clothes make a high and aromatic pile on the floor. Francesca and I play Laundry Chicken, to see which one of us breaks down first and washes the clothes. I suspect that at the middle of the pile is a kitten. Two kittens.

Still, no matter what, I refuse to iron. Nor do I want her to iron. In fact, I don't own an iron and will not buy one. Women shouldn't iron, ever. It's our wrinkles that make us interesting.

And there's a drastic difference in Francesca's and my hours. I keep Normal Hours, and she keeps Vampire Hours. I used to wait up for her and worry. Now I go to sleep and hope for the best. Even when she stays home, she's up late watching TV or talking on the cell phone. Did you know that at any given hour of the night, three billion sleepless young people are updating their Facebook profile, friending each other, or announcing their newly single status? If only we could harness their energy, we'd be less dependent on foreign oil.

Our entertainment choices differ, too. I don't go out much, but last weekend, I suggested that we go see a movie at seven thirty. She talked me into seeing the ten-thirty show. I fell asleep in the movie, twice, and she had the gall to wake me up. What does it mean if even Brad Pitt puts me to sleep?

Don't answer.

Plus she bought a box of fresh Raisinets and a bag of popcorn, which reminded me that carbs practically demand to be eaten, so now I've fallen off the wagon.

You get the idea. My daughter has disturbed my empty nest and she'll be home all summer.

And you know what?

I wouldn't have it any other way.

FASHIONISTA

I'm not sure when I officially stopped mattering, but I think it began at age 40. I know this because I'm a great reader of fashion magazines, and *InStyle* recently told me that I no longer mattered, if indeed I existed at all.

They didn't even let me down easy. And I subscribe.

The article I was reading was called "Great At Any Age." It was about beauty tips for women as they got older, and the article was broken down by age groups. The first page was addressed to women in their 20s and told them that "nothing topical gets rid of cellulite completely."

Funny, I can remember my 20s, and it was the one decade of my life that I didn't have cellulite. I had an orange Mazda, my first VISA card, and several thousand law school applications, but no cellulite.

Never mind. I turned the page.

The second page was addressed to women in their 30s and informed them that their "skin was thinning." That didn't ring true to me, either. Every woman knows that as she gets older, her skin doesn't get thinner. On the contrary, it gets thicker. Those of us who used to be thin-skinned simply stop caring about what people think of what we say, write, do, or wear. I always thought this was called perspective, but boy, was I wrong. *InStyle* told me so.

I turned to the next page, which was addressed to women in their "40s+" and told them that "gentle exfoliation" would stimulate their circulation "for a smoothing effect." I wasn't worried that I wasn't smooth, but nevertheless, I resolved instantly to start exfoliating and to be gentle about it.

I turned the page. But there were no more age groups in the "Great At Any Age" article.

The "Great At Any Age" article was over.

The top age limit to be Great At was 40s+.

Now, wait.

I had thought I was Great At Any Age, because that's what they told me at the top of the page. But they really didn't mean it. I was Great Only At The Ages of 20 Through 40. They were the only gals who got their own age categories, instead of being lumped in all together. What about the ages of 42, 47, 52, 65, 75, 79, 83, and older? At those ages, I wasn't Great. I might actually Suck.

The article should have been called: "Sucking At Any Age Over 40."

I flipped the page and tried not to take it too much to heart. After all, as I say, my skin is thicker now, and nothing bothers me anymore.

The next article was entitled, "How to Wear . . . a Sporty Jacket." The ellipsis are theirs. Don't ask me why. I'm 40s+ and can barely take care of myself in the bathroom. Ask a twenty-year-old with cellulite.

Anyway, I was excited when I saw the article about how to wear . . . a sporty jacket. I'd never thought about how to wear . . . a sporty jacket. I had always assumed that you . . . put your arms in the sleeves and slipped it . . . over your shoulders.

But what do I know?

I was eager to learn about sporty jackets.

Only one problem. The sporty jacket article was addressed to age groups, too. Since when does a sporty jacket come with age limits? This is America. I always thought I could wear . . . a sporty jacket at any age.

Boy, was I wrong. Again!

Unbeknownst to me, sporty jackets had a shelf life. In fact, *I* had a shelf life. I'd thought if I was alive, I mattered, but *In-Style* set me straight.

Oddly, the age groups for sporty jackets were different than the age groups for cellulite creams. The first page of the article pictured a sporty jacket with a hoodie, for women in their "20s/30s." The second page showed the same jacket with a white shirt for women, in their "30s/40s." The third page showed the jacket with a set of plastic beads, for women in their "40s/50s."

Whew. What a relief. A number with a 5 in front. I did exist, at least as far as sporty jackets were concerned.

But I was confused. I existed for sporty jacket purposes but not for cellulite cream purposes. Doesn't this seem backwards? I don't want to reveal too much, but my 40s+ self has more need for a cellulite cream than a sporty jacket. Unless the jacket is sporty enough to cover my tushie.

Plus, the article raised new questions. Am I too old for my handbag? Too young for my ballet flats? Are my clothes snickering at me behind my back?

Then I thought of something. *InStyle* didn't ask me my age when they cashed my

check for the subscription.
  Ya think they'll ask when I cancel?

HOLLOW BUNNIES

I'm wary of writing about religion, and though I want to say a word about Easter and Passover here, you'll see that the following has more to do with saturated fats than Christianity or Judaism.

I was raised in a family that qualified as the Worst Catholics in the World. We didn't go to church because my mother was excommunicated, since she had been divorced before she married my father. And if my mother wasn't going to church, none of us was. As a child, I understood only that the Church didn't like my mother, and since I loved her, I was on her side. So for me, Easter was about chocolate.

And plastic.

What I remember about Easter morning was that my brother Frank and I got a pink plastic basket full of green plastic grass. Nestled within were chocolate eggs from Woolworth's, cream-filled, and a huge chocolate bunny, unfortunately hollow, because we were on the low-rent side.

I feel nostalgic for those multi-colored mornings, for neon-orange peanuts and chrome-yellow Peeps. For fat jellybeans, from before there were "gourmet" jellybeans that taste like popcorn or daiquiris, which is against nature. When I was little, all jelly-beans tasted the same.

Like sugar, as God intended.

The only jellybeans I really wanted were the cherry ones that washed your teeth in a scary red juice, or the licorice ones that blackened your tongue like a chow's.

We also got dressed up on Easter morn-ing, and there are plenty of pictures of me looking stiff in a crinoline dress and brother Frank in a little gray suit, a red bowtie, and short pants with knee socks, topped off with a round cap that had a chin strap. Much later, we would learn that Frank was gay, and I still maintain we should have been tipped off by that Easter get-up.

I can get nostalgic about every Easter memory but the spray-painted chick. Spray-painted chicks were a big thing in my old neighborhood. I still can't imagine what anybody was thinking, to do something so cruel as to take a live baby chick and dye it an "Easter" color. But my parents fell for this every year and they'd buy us a red, green, or purple chick. The novelty would wear off in an hour, not coincidentally with the sugar crash, and then nobody seemed to know what to do with the poor chick.

Our red chick and our green chick died in short order, but the purple chick, against all odds, didn't die after the first week. Or even the second. Of course, we had no idea how to raise him. We fed him Cheerios and meatballs. We covered the floor of our bedroom with newspaper and kept him there. In time, he lost his purple feathers and grew to be a chubby brown chicken, whom we named Herman. He had a friendly personality, hanging out with us and walking through our legs like a house cat. He lived a full year, and when he died, we cried so hard that it made Easter the anniversary of his death, rather than the resurrection of anything else.

When I got older, we moved to a neighborhood that was predominantly Jewish. I got invited to bar and bat mitzvahs, and I learned that Jews celebrated Passover. My best friend Rachel kept the traditional fast on the first day. I didn't understand Judaism much better than I understood Catholicism, but her family invited me to their seder, where I had a great time and got to

73

ask a question, which I didn't understand either.

But what I did understand about Passover was that Rachel's family was together around a full and lovely table — two wonderful parents, three fun-loving brothers, and my best friend in the world — all joking around with each other, laughing, and inviting me into their family. And to this day, I still am in their family, as they are in mine.

To me, that's what every holiday is all about.

That's even what every religion is about.

Love.

EMPOWERMENT

Nowadays, superpowers are everywhere. At the movies, Spider-Man has superpowers, and so do Iron Man, Sandman, Venom, and whatever the other bad guy is. On TV, all the people in *Heroes* have superpowers, and *Medium* is a soccer mom with superpowers. In books, Harry Potter is a boy with superpowers, and Tolkien's *The Children of Hurin* has hobbits with superpowers, which may be redundant.

Something is happening in pop culture. I'm no detective, but I think it's that people want superpowers.

Not me, though. I don't want superpowers. I don't want to turn people into sand; I like them the way they are, at least the ones I didn't divorce.

And I don't want to spin webs out of my fingertips. I'd settle for ten really nice fingernails, all at the same time.

Come to think of it, instead of superpowers, I'd want normal powers. You may know that I'm picky about really important things, like Splenda and croutons. But I'm flexible on powers. I'd settle for everyday powers. Things that normal people can do, but I can't.

Right off the top of my head, I can make a wish list of ten normal powers that would change my life:

1. The power to match a lid to its travel mug. They say every pot has a lid, but every travel mug clearly does not. I have three hundred black plastic lids in my cabinet and none of them fit any of my travel mugs. I can't find the right lid, ever. And I never, ever will. This is not a metaphor for my social life.

2. The power to remember the directions that somebody tells me after I pull over to ask for them. Every time, as soon as I drive away, I forget. This phenomenon is impossible to explain, especially considering that I remember the words to every high school cheer. Push 'em back, shove 'em back, waaay back! See?

3. The power to eat anything I want

and not gain weight. If I had this power, I'd fly around in my cape and protect us all from Kirstie Alley.

4. The power to stop my hair from frizzing. I know it's wrong to base your self-esteem on your hair, but let's get real. Good hair helps. I went on a vacation to Paris, and my hair looked terrific. France has no humidity. A good hair country!

5. The power to find my keys and cell phone at will. In fact, if my cell phone could call my car keys, that would work, too.

6. The power to walk in slingbacks without the strap falling down in back. This is an often-overlooked normal power. Anybody can walk in heels. Only experts can walk in slingbacks. I don't qualify. Yet.

7. The power to watch *Grey's Anatomy* without being totally annoyed by Ellen Pompeo's lips. Lip actresses drive me nuts. I was barely over Calista Flockhart in *Ally McBeal,* and now this. Renée Zellweger, watch out. I'm taking you down, girl.

8. The power to stay awake until the

end of *The Colbert Report.* This is no reflection on Stephen Colbert, who knows that I love him because I tell him every night, telepathically. (Okay, borderline creepy.) Yet I barely make it through The Word. I can't stay awake as late as I used to. Again, no reflection on my social life, real or imagined. (With you, Stephen, only you.)

9. The power to apply liquid eyeliner without it coming out like a sales chart. I feel sure that my life would change if I could put on liquid liner. Best friend Franca can do it and she looks great. Daughter Francesca can do it, too. Even Paris Hilton can do it. I've been trying and failing to accomplish this for the past twenty years. Now it's probably too late, because my eyelids have fallen like the final curtain.

10. Finally, there's an array of normal powers that I'm squeezing in here, while I'm making my wish list. I'd love the power to get the Christmas lights working on the first try, find my dry cleaning receipt when I need it, remember where I parked my car, return the DVD rental

before the late charges reach $37, and locate a working pen while I'm on the phone — and a working flashlight when the power goes out.

Is it so much to ask?
I don't want to be Superwoman. Just Normalwoman!
Ka-POW!

BETTY AND VERONICA

I realized the other day that I don't care about superpowers because I didn't read those comics as a kid. To me, Superman and Batman were for boys. Girls had Betty Cooper and Veronica Lodge, the blonde and brunette bombshells of the Archie comics. I loved those comics and still remember their many valuable lessons.

What were they?

Here's Betty and Veronica's Lessons For Girls.

Before we begin, let me remind you that Betty and Veronica were best friends who went to Riverdale High School. They were both gorgeous, impossibly curvy, and permanently seventeen.

But their personalities were very different:

Betty was poor, but nice and natural. She wore her canary-yellow hair in a bouncy ponytail and dressed like a tomboy. In fact, Betty has her own webpage these days, which reveals that she sews her own clothes. The website sums her up as "your average small town girl," and her blog (of course, she has a blog) contains salsa recipes.

In contrast, Veronica had money, and was mean and spoiled. The website says that she's "gorgeous, sophisticated, sexy and very RICH." (The capitals are theirs; I save my capitals for better things.) Veronica is also "ambitious" and "confident." Veronica writes in her blog: "only three weeks of school left — must buy summer clothes!"

By the way, neither girl is described as smart. Anywhere.

What have we learned, so far?

Lesson One: Poor people are better than rich people. Blond people are better than brunette people. Black people don't exist.

Unlike Betty, who lives with her normal family, Veronica lives with her father, a family situation which is borderline creepy. Mr. Lodge is most often found sitting in a club chair, reading the newspaper and waiting for his daughter to ask him for things. She calls him Daddykins. He always says yes.

Lesson Two: Single parents pro-

81

duce messed-up kids.

Betty and Veronica form the distaff base of a love triangle that peaks in Archie Andrews. The storyline of every comic is the same — Betty and Veronica, theoretically best friends, scheme, plot, and deceive each other in order to win Archie.

Lesson Three: Even your best friend can, and should, be ditched for a guy.

Which girl do you think Archie chooses more often — sweet, uncomplicated Betty or neurotic but sexy Veronica? You guessed it.

Lesson Four: Men dig crazy.

The website admits that: "Betty is extremely devoted to Archie, but sadly is most often playing second fiddle to her best friend Veronica for his affections. Through every crazy loving scheme to win Archie's love, Betty always remains completely unaffected, loyal and sweet." Of course she does. How Betty of her.

Lesson Five: Nice is a waste of time.

But here's something I never understood. Why do Betty and Veronica want Archie so much? He's not attractive. His hair is orange, parted in the middle, and he has crosshatches for sideburns. His nose looks like a jellybean.

Lesson Six: Any boyfriend is better than no boyfriend at all.
Archie doesn't even have a good personality. He's not smart, and that's fine with him. The website doesn't apologize for the fact that he "brings home average grades from school." On the contrary, in all respects, Archie is a "typical small town boy."

Lesson Seven: Mediocrity rocks!
But Archie does have a "good, solid family background."

Lesson Eight: Learn to settle.
So, growing up, who did I want to be — Betty or Veronica? I'll tell the truth. I knew I was supposed to want to be Betty, but I secretly wanted to be Veronica.

Lesson Nine: It's okay to be superficial.
It didn't matter what Betty or Veronica

wanted to be when they grew up. In the comics I remembered, they didn't want to be anything but with Archie. However, the website has more recently assigned them career aspirations, because women have the vote now.

Lesson Ten: History can always be revised. If you remember it otherwise, you're wrong.

So, what are the career goals of these two? The site says, "Veronica would someday like to run Lodge Enterprises." Presumably that's her father's business, or a Mafia front. Knowing Veronica as I do, I wouldn't put it past her. Veronica could be an excellent crime lord if she'd stay out of Neiman Marcus.

Lesson Eleven: Nepotism is a fancy word for born winner.

Finally, what's Betty's career plan? "Betty's goal is to become a famous writer."

Lesson Twelve: Follow your dream, in case you're a Betty.

ODE TO PARENTS OF COLLEGE-AGE KIDS

My baby bird, daughter Francesca, is home from college for the summer, and I thought it would be fun for you to hear from her. I hope the following will help my fellow parental units to see how our college-age kids (sorry, adults) see us. So, below is from Francesca:

Now that I'm older, I imagined that living at home with my mother would be different. Not that it needed to change; we've always had the best relationship. I can honestly say that my mom is my best friend. But now that I'm twenty-one, I figured our dynamic would be more mature.

Not exactly.

My childhood nickname was Kiki, and my mom always had hundreds of nonsensical pet-names for me. The days of BooBoo, Baby Bumpy, and Mocha JaMocha are over. Or so I thought.

We were in the shoe department, trying to be cool (we both inexplicably get dressed up to go to the mall) when my mom looked up from the sandals and said, "Hey, Bumpy! Look at these!" I resorted to the oh-so-teenage, *"Mo-om."* We totally blew our grown-up cover.

Back home, one change in our interaction wasn't due to *my* age, it was due to hers. She'd read that she should drink red wine for her heart, so one night, she poured herself a glass and offered me one, too.

This alone was a big step. My mother doesn't drink, and when I was younger, she decried the perils of alcohol with Prohibition-era ferocity. So, as she poured me a glass of wine, I felt as if we had turned a corner in our new, mature relationship.

I made sure to not drink more than one glass, but I wasn't the one who had to be worried. After just a few sips, she started up: "Oh I feel it. I can feel it already. Can you feel it?" she asked, excitedly. And before my mom had even finished the glass, she was declaring, "I'm drunk!" like a trium-phant frat boy. My mom's night of boozing (still only one glass) quickly turned sour. She complained the whole night: "Ugh, I have a headache from that wine. I'm sleepy from that wine. I can't sleep from that wine." She required more post-party care than my freshman-year roommate.

Jeez, Mom, grow up.

But then, I'm not exactly the sophisticate I thought I'd be when it comes to our mother-daughter time. I'm embarrassed to admit that there are still moments when I'm embarrassed to be out with Mom. This is crazy, because she's great, and I love spending time with her. But even as a grown (or nearly) woman, the shadow of an insecure thirteen-year-old follows me around. Like last week, I persuaded my mom to see a movie at ten-thirty, because secretly I knew the theater would be less crowded then, and it would be less likely that someone I knew would catch me on date-night with Mom. As it happened, I did run into an old friend from high school who was there on an actual date. Busted.

But it's not just at the movies. Last week she gave me a ride to my doctor's appointment. I had a wart on my toe removed and also got the HPV vaccine, Gardasil. As we were checking out, my mom was being her usual friendly self, updating the receptionist on my life. It used to bother teenage-me when she shared the details of my life, but now I see it's just love. And anyway, what could she really say?

"Today she got that Gardasil shot and got rid of those nasty warts!" Mom chirped. I cringed.

My mother has a way with words.

But truly, I'm lucky that I feel so close to my mom. We can talk about anything — even sex. In fact, it was her idea for me to get the HPV vaccine.

We've come a long way. When my mom was moving me out of my freshman year dorm, I was mortified that she found condoms in my nightstand. If that happened this year, it wouldn't matter. I'm old enough to know what's in a woman's nightstand is her business.

That's why I'm never, ever, looking in hers.

I'm not old enough.

Right, kid, now go empty the dishwasher.

What Francesca doesn't realize is that she'll always be my baby, no matter what age. But I have to admit, she's grown into an incredible young woman who is everything I hoped she would be: smart, strong, funny, and loving. As you can see, she does tell the truth.

And now, she's grounded.

FAMILY FUN

Mother Mary and Brother Frank are here to visit, spending a week at my house, and I learned a few things you might be able to use when your own family comes to visit. By the way, let's all stipulate at the outset that I love my family, even if it doesn't sound like I do, below. But I like to keep it real, so what follows is the light side of the dark side of family visits, if you follow.

That said, here are my Top Ten Tips to Family Fun:

1. **You can't chloroform your mother.** What happened was that I wanted to take my mother to see the new movie about Edith Piaf. My mother loves Edith Piaf and is, in fact, the only person I ever met who knows who Edith Piaf is. When I heard that there was a movie about Edith Piaf, I thought it would

be perfect for her. Only problem was, the movie theater was In Town, and my mother wouldn't go In Town to see a movie, even one about Edith Piaf. We fought about it, and I considered chloroforming her and taking her there, but my brother said I couldn't. So don't do it. If your brother's around.

2. **Watching eggs cook makes them cook faster.** One morning, I was making fried eggs for breakfast, and my brother thought I should turn up the heat. I disagreed. We fought about it, after which he sat in stony silence and watched the eggs fry. You know what? They fried super-fast. In fact, I think he fried them with his eyes. Grab your brother and try this at home. Fight first.

3. **Too many cooks spoil the tomato sauce.** My mother and I tried to make one dinner together in my nice big kitchen, which was when I learned that no kitchen is big enough for two women to make dinner in, especially if they are blood relatives. And especially if they are mother and daughter. Take it from me, fighting will follow. And

if a granddaughter joins them, something will explode. All that will remain is a small pile of dried oregano.

4. **Getting four people into a car to drive to a restaurant takes as long as a full-scale expedition to Nepal, including sherpas.** After our cooking fiasco, I thought reservations would be the answer, but I simply couldn't get four people to move to the car and get inside. I kept saying "are you ready yet" or "let's go" or "time to rock" or "everybody outta the pool." We were late for our reservation and had to wait for another table, which was when I learned that encouragement won't make your family go faster, but slower. This is like the frying eggs, only the opposite, if you follow.

5. **Family math is different from normal math.** There is a mathematical relationship between the number of people in the house and the number of times you run the dishwasher, but that relationship is exponential. By this I mean, if you have two (2) new people in the

house, for a total of four (4) people, you would guess that you'd have to run the dishwasher an extra time a day. Maybe two (2) times, at the most. But if you guess that, you'd be wrong. I learned you'll have to run the dishwasher 362.5 times a day. (!) The .5 is what puts it over the top.

6. **In a related tip, two extra people will produce 481 extra bags of garbage.** I saw this with my own eyes. And the number of people agreeing to take out the trash will always equal zero. (0).

7. **Crossword puzzles are crack cocaine for mothers.** Every morning of her visit, my mother does crossword and moves on to jumbles, cryptoquotes, and word searches. She doesn't look up until she's finished. I supply her with coffee, but all I see is the top of her little gray head. My brother tells me this means she is happy. So, when your family visits and your mother is acting up and you can't chloroform her, now you know what to do.

8. **There is an inverse relationship between dieting and eating.** This

is another one of those funky family math things. By this I mean, the more people in your house on a diet, the more often they will eat. So, in our case, we're all on a diet, yet we eat all day long. However, we talk about our diet incessantly. That's how you lose the weight. Keep talking.

9. **Rain is your enemy.** You know what I mean. If it's sunny, everybody can go to neutral corners, i.e., go outside or walk the dogs. But if it rains, you're all inside together in the family room, fighting over what to watch on TV, having fought over which movie to rent and deciding to let the whole thing go. In the end, you will end up in front of a continuous loop of *Everybody Loves Raymond,* and you will welcome it, because at least it's not *Matlock.*

10. **In between the family fighting, there will be brief periods of harmony and even love, however unexpected.** For example, my mother and daughter bonded over their shared dislike of Jennifer Anniston. This came as a major surprise, at least from my mother,

because Jennifer Aniston is Telly Savalas's goddaughter and my mother loves Telly Savalas.

Even so, she wouldn't go In Town for him.

CORGI, INTERRUPTED

It's come to this: my dog is on Prozac. Yes, you read that right. Ruby, my Pembroke Welsh corgi, is on Prozac. Laugh away. Tell me I must be crazy to put a dog on meds. My only defense is that talk therapy didn't work.

Let me explain.

You may remember that I have four dogs: three golden retrievers and Ruby The Corgi. Anyone with even a passing knowledge of dogs would know that between three goldens and a corgi, it would be the corgi who would end up on a controlled substance.

My pets are like that *Sesame Street* song, "One of These Things Is Not Like The Others." Here is what the goldens are like: fun, easy, friendly, happy, and loving, on a continuous loop. You could have three goldens in the room and not know it. They love to sleep. They love everything. Honestly, I kept adding goldens because I forgot they were there. You could be sitting in a roomful of goldens and think to yourself, You know, we need a dog.

The corgi is Not Like The Others. Here is what the corgi is like: sensitive, alert, watchful, picky, and feisty. If she's in the room, you know it. In fact, you're probably obeying her. Corgis are low to the ground, dwarf dogs bred to herd cattle, and Ruby has been known to herd the goldens, me, my daughter, and also, on occasion, the UPS guy. How Ruby knows what she was bred to do, way back in Wales three thousand years ago, is beyond me. I got her at Christmas, after daughter Francesca had gone off to college. Ruby was intended to replace Francesca, which is not working out exactly as planned. How many parents can say that their dog is on drugs, but their kid isn't?

To get back to the story, Ruby used to be a wonderful and funny dog, but she recently morphed into The Terrifying Biting Attacking Dwarf. In the summer of the movie *Transformers,* Ruby got transformed. She's like *Saw,* with paws. For some reason, she began to start fights with the oldest golden, Lucy, whenever that sweet old dog ambled into the kitchen, took a nap, or committed an otherwise unpardonable offense.

I admit to you, I didn't handle this well.

I'm the mother of only one child, so I have no idea what to do when my kids fight. I don't know how people with more than one child handle this problem. I thought back to what my mother used to say, when she had to break up a fight between brother Frank and me, so I tried screaming, "Separate, you two!" But it didn't work.

Also, "Stop or I'll turn this car around." But it didn't apply.

Then I remembered that when we were really bad, my mother would take off her shoe and throw it at us. But I'm beyond that. Also, I missed.

So Francesca and I took Ruby to the vet, who suggested that maybe the fighting was happening because Ruby realizes that Lucy is getting older and therefore losing her position as leader of the pack. Evidently, Ruby wants to be the new boss, and will bite and chew her way to the top. She's Donald Trump on four legs.

The sad part is that good old Lucy doesn't care who's leader of the pack. No golden does, at least none of mine. They say: You wanna lead the pack? Knock yourself out. I'm going back to sleep. You won't even know I'm here.

So we tried to manage the problem, with lots of no's, daily walks, and some calm assertiveness learned from TV's Cesar Milan, The Dog Whisperer. I used to watch his show for fun; now I watch it like homework. I read his book. I bought the special Illusion collar, which I can't figure out how to put on.

But in the end, I turned to drugs. Ruby is now on ten milligrams of Prozac, twice day.

Soon, she'll be in Ruhab.

NATURE GIRL

I'm a big fan of nature. I enjoy walking through the grass with my dogs, or riding little Buddy through the woods. Also I like to look through the window at a cloudless blue sky, pretty as a Microsoft screensaver. In other words, I like nature just fine, as long as it stays outside.

But lately at my house, nature has been overstepping her bounds.

It began at the first dip in the temperature, and to me, it's no coincidence that it happened at football season. For some reason, around this time of year, every time I open my front door, spiders try to run inside my house. I'm not kidding. It's as if the spiders have been huddling out front, and the sound of the doorknob is their hut-hut-hut signal. I open the door and, instantly, spiders charge over the threshold at me, in a flying spider wedge formation. I'm not talking only one or two spiders; I'm talking about six or seven spiders, and they're huge, like spider linebackers in a Super Bowl team of arachnids.

I have no defense.

I can't bring myself to kill them, because I couldn't take the guilt. I learned somewhere along the line that spiders are good for us and blah blah blah. Even if I were less of a goody-goody, it would be impossible to kill them all. It would be like playing whack-a-mole, and four or five of them would run through my legs, which they consider mere goal posts to scoring a spider touchdown. Sometimes they have to settle for a spider field goal, which is when they reach the floor vents and disappear inside. By October, my heating ducts will be full of webs, the perfect decoration for their big Halloween party.

Back in the summer, or preseason, when only one or two spiders played for the team, I was able to defend my end of the field by turning a glass tumbler over them, then slipping a magazine underneath the tumbler and taking them back outside, where they belong. Another defense that worked was cursing and stamping my feet, because they seemed to react to hysteria and/or profanity. They would simply turn around, run outside, and regroup for the next play. But my tumbler defense won't work anymore; I don't have the coordination, or the glassware.

The current score is Spiders 52, Scottoline 0. They even improved their record from last season and while they claim they made some excellent trades, I smell steroids.

Either way, I know when I'm licked, and my only solution was to stop using my front door. Now I go out the back door all the time, which is completely inconvenient, not to mention embarrassing. I save face only by telling myself that I have outsmarted the spiders, at least until they resort to battering rams of praying mantises.

But it gets worse.

The other day, I came home and in the kitchen was my adorable gray-and-white kitten, Vivi, resting like a baby Sphinx — in front of a long green snake, which lay motionless on the floor. I went into my hysteria-and-profanity routine, but, to my horror, it awakened both kitten and snake. The snake slithered at warp speed over the Karastan and through the kitchen chairs. Vivi took off after the snake, and I took off after Vivi.

There ensued chasing (Vivi) and wriggling (snake) and screaming (me). Somehow I scooped Vivi up and threw her into the bathroom, then I screamed some more while the snake undulated around the kitchen, its green head raised like a suburban cobra.

By the way, no other pets came to my aid. The other kitten scooted off, her black tail a question mark, and my three golden retrievers lolled sleepily on the kitchen floor, though I could tell they were rooting for me, inside. Ruby The Corgi pointed and laughed, which means that I'm cutting her Prozac.

I didn't know what to do. If I couldn't bring myself to kill a spider, there was no way I could bring myself to kill a snake. I wouldn't know how, anyway. Step on it? You can only ask so much of a clog.

I ran to the closet, grabbed a broom, and, screaming the entire time, swept the snake out of the house, through the front door.

The snake was only too glad to slither outside.

The spiders were only too glad to run inside.

Touchdown!

KING TUT

Okay, so my brother has escaped back to Miami, and my mother is extending her visit with me and daughter Francesca. One afternoon we were all in front of the TV, comatose before the *Everybody Loves Raymond* marathon, having finished the *Law & Order* marathon. For the past two weeks, my mother wouldn't go anywhere else but the kitchen. Driven to distraction, I offhandedly suggested we go see the King Tut exhibit.

"King Tut?" my mother asked, suddenly perking up. Her eyes widened behind her round glasses like an octogenarian Harry Potter. "Let's go!"

I blinked, astounded. "But, Ma, it's In Town."

"So what? I love King Tut!"

I didn't say what I was thinking, which was, *More than Telly Savalas?*

"Only thing is, he's not there," my

mother said.

"That's because he's dead," I told her, then ordered the tickets online before she remembered she didn't like having fun.

The next day, we were at the King Tut exhibit — Mother Mary, daughter Francesca, and me — three generations of Scottoline women, freshly showered and dressed up, giddy to be out of the house. My mother wore her best perfume, smelling great because she stopped smoking a few years ago, when she got throat cancer. She's in complete remission now, which doesn't surprise me. It'll take more than a deadly disease to kill Mother Mary. I'm betting on a meteor.

I picked up our tickets, bought the audio tour, and slipped the headphones over my mother's hearing aid, then turned on her audiotape, which was narrated by Omar Sharif. She broke into a sly smile and said, "Omar Sharif can park his slippers next to mine anytime."

"Who's Omar Sharif?" Francesca asked.

"Doctor Zhivago," my mother answered.

"Nicky Arnstein," I added.

"Who?" Francesca asked again, and we let it go. I cannot explain Omar Sharif to a generation who has not swooned over him. For Omar Sharif, I would have learned to play bridge.

But back to the story.

We waited in a line that zigzagged for an hour, which was a lot of standing for Mother Mary, especially after she'd come three blocks from the parking garage. She'd walked only slowly, but she hadn't complained at all. Her vision is poor from glaucoma and macular degeneration, but she was gamely squinting at the museum map. We entered the exhibit, which began with a short movie about King Tut. In the dark, my mother said to me, "Watch your purse."

In the first room of the exhibit, we were a field trip of underachievers. We couldn't pronounce Tutankhamen or figure out his genealogy, and we didn't know what canopic meant. I kept pressing the wrong numbers on my mother's gadget for the audio tour, so the tape would play the spiel about liver embalming when she was looking at the mask of Nefertiti.

But we found our stride as the exhibit continued. The lights were low and dramatic; the rooms modeled after the King's own tomb. I held onto my mother's elbow as she wobbled along, and my daughter read aloud for her the plaques she couldn't read herself.

We saw lovely calcite jars, so luminous that they glowed. Delicate statues called *shabti,* glazed a vibrant blue. A gilded chest covered with carved hieroglyphs. The artifacts, all over three thousand years old, had been placed in King Tut's tomb to keep him company in the afterlife. In the Egyptian culture's reverence for the dead, I could see its reverence for the living. Looking at the amazing artifacts, holding onto my mother and my daughter, I realized that this moment might never come again. Cancer kills mothers every day, and death comes for all, boy kings and perfumed women.

Then I tried to understand why it took a glimpse of the afterlife to make me appreciate this life.

It was an afterlife lesson.

We passed into the last room of the exhibit, which was darker than all the others. I had expected to see the grand finale, King Tut's famous golden sarcophagus. But where it should have been, instead was a stand the approximate size and shape of a sarcophagus. On it was projected a ghostly photo of King Tut, which morphed from a picture of his mummified remains to a picture of his sarcophagus.

"What's this?" I asked, mystified. "Where's King Tut?"

Mother Mary said, "Told you. He's not here. I read it in the paper."

"*That's* what you meant?"

"Yes."

I felt terrible, for my mother. "Sorry about that."

But she waved me off. "Makes no difference."

Francesca looked over at me. "Bummed, Mom?"

"No," I answered, without hesitation.

"Me, neither," she said, with a smile

And we both took Mother Mary by the arm.

Dream Job

It's fun to do something dumb. Not something really dumb, like my second marriage. That was really *really* dumb.

I mean, it's fun to perform a mindless task. I realized this today, when I clipped my pony. Yes, even though I'm a grown-up, I have a pony named Buddy. I bought him from a little girl who thought he was too old, too small, and too slow.

Bingo!

Buddy is a brown-and-white paint with a wavy black mane and eyes round as Ping-Pong balls. He's barely taller than a golden retriever, and when I ride him, my heels practically drag on the ground. And he's shaggier than a mastodon. He needs to be clipped twice a summer, which is where our adventure begins.

I was supposed to be working on a novel at the time, but I couldn't figure out the plot, the character, or the dialogue. That's about all there is to one of my books, except for the sex scene, but we'll leave that for another day. I was in first draft, and even though I tell myself first draft doesn't have to be perfect, I feel as if it does. By the time my book goes out the door, it has to be as perfect as I can make it, which still isn't perfect. It's perfect, for me.

But today I couldn't do perfect; I couldn't even do good. I lost my mojo, it was hot outside, and I knew a pony who was sweating his ass off. So I went to the barn, turned on the Rolling Stones, tied that little furball up in the aisle, and grabbed the electric clippers.

Start me up.

I shaved strips into Buddy's thick, curly hair, and the Stones got me rocking. My mind wandered, and I became Mick Jagger. I sang. I played air guitar. I looked awesome in really tight pants.

Two hours later, my little Beast of Burden looked as if he'd been sheared by Keith Richards. Mental patients get better haircuts, and a close second are condemned prisoners. My clipping method wasn't perfect. Buddy's coat had been matted in places, but I cut it off rather than untangle it. Nor had I decided in advance which type of clip job to give him, and there are three types: full body clip (self-explanatory), trace clip (top-half only), and Scottoline clip (until pony looks schizophrenic).

And the worst part was that I had started the job wearing my prescription sunglasses instead of my regular glasses, but that had made it too dark to see what I was doing. So I took the sunglasses off, but then I couldn't see the pony at all. Still I clipped him anyway. I got the job done, which is good enough for a rock star.

The other mindless task I love is mowing the lawn. I mow on an ancient diesel tractor and I pretend it's a new John Deere riding mower. Or a Corvette, a Maserati, or a horse that's taller, faster, and younger than Buddy. I'm in the ring at a horse show. In my mind.

A girl can dream, can't she?

And I don't do a perfect job on the lawn, either. I ride my tractor/Olympic steed around the backyard, plowing strips wherever I please, spewing chopped sticks and broken glass. I breathe in random scents of mint, onion grass, and diesel smoke. Bugs fly up my nose, and I wear orange earphones for maximum hotness.

I aim only to get the job done. I swerve to avoid frogs, which creates crop circles worthy of M. Night Shyamalan. I drive around rocks that have been there forever, and my backyard looks like it has hairy moles. So what? My Aunt Rachel had hairy moles, and she was my favorite.

And if a hose is on the ground, I drive around that, too. I never get off the tractor, move the hose, and mow underneath it. I leave my hose and grass to their own devices. Not everything on my property is my business.

And, as you may have guessed, I never decide in advance what type of mowing method to use. As you know, there are three types: up and down (self-explanatory), around and around (dizzying), or Scottoline (surprise me!)

But here is the point. What I do during these mindless tasks is dream. Some people call them chores, but to me, they're dream jobs. This isn't just marketing or reverse psychology; we all need time to dream. I take a break from the real job to do the dream job. And unlike the real job, the dream job doesn't have it be perfect. It just has to get done in a dreamy way.

And after I clipped Buddy today, I went inside, sat down at my computer, and got back to work. Do you think my plot, characters, and dialogue magically appeared?

You must be dreaming.

SUGGESTION BOX

I don't know when this started, but I've become very suggestible lately. I first noticed it when I was watching TV and a commercial came on, for spaghetti and meatballs. Instantly I wanted a plate of spaghetti and meatballs. I couldn't help myself. I craved spaghetti and meatballs, even though eating carbs is now against federal law and I'm supposed to be a vegetarian. Still, I spent a lot of time fantasizing about spaghetti and meatballs.

Then it got worse.

I was watching *Sex and the City* reruns, and I wanted a nice pink Cosmo, or three. During a Wendy's commercial, I wanted a square hamburger. And every time Kentucky Fried Chicken came on TV, I'd be thinking, extra crispy is the best. Extra crispy always hits the spot. I'd just love me some extra crispy right about now.

But it went beyond food.

I'd watch tennis on TV, and I'd want to be a professional tennis player. I'd watch *Top Chef,* and I'd want to cook for Chef Tom Colicchio. Bottom line, I'm starting to want whatever I see on television, and lately I'm watching *Miami Ink.*

You can see where this is going.

Miami Ink is a reality show about people who go to this tattoo parlor in Miami and walk out covered with tattoos. There's a little story behind each person's tattoo, and many of the stories are sad. There are parents who get tattoos to memorialize children who died; there are teenagers who get tattoos to memorialize parents who died. Plenty of people get tattoos of their dogs and cats who died. All this dying and all this tattooing, I can't take it. I cry like a baby through every episode.

But that's beside the point. The point is that I went from being a person who was disgusted by tattoos to being a person who wants tattoos very badly.

I think about tattoos all the time now. I look at pictures in magazines and wonder, would that would make a nice tattoo? I squint at tattoos on other people, appraising them with a critical eye. I visits websites with tattoos when I'm supposed to be working. I think about tattoos so much that I

113

have already selected three, though they are imaginary.

And because I have to decide where to put my three imaginary tattoos, I think about that, too. Should they go on my arms? Too flabby. Lower back? No tramp stamp for me. Ankle? Looks like dirt with heels. Neck? Can you say state prison?

There are a lot of choices to be made in the imaginary world in which I live.

I suspect, however, that I'm not the only person to pick out imaginary tattoos. Fess up. You know you want one. If you tell me yours, I'll tell you mine:

I like Kewpie dolls, so for my first tattoo, I thought it would be nice to have a tiny little Kewpie doll on the inside of my wrist, where it will be discreet, even classy. (Okay, maybe not classy.)

For my second tattoo, I would like an old-fashioned Sacred Heart, but I don't know where on my body to put a Sacred Heart tattoo. It's too butch for my arm, and I could burn in hell if I put it anyplace else. You take your chances with the religious tattoos, and you don't want to be thumbing your nose at you-know-who.

Thirdly, I think one of those colorful Japanese scenes would be nice, something with orange koi fish or calcium-white kabuki masks or an ornate kimono of threaded gold. I can't decide about my last tattoo. I think about it a lot. It has replaced spaghetti and meatballs in my magical thinking, at least for the time being.

Unfortunately, I've passed my suggestibility on to daughter Francesca. We watch *Miami Ink* together, and though she doesn't want a tattoo, she wants the tattoo artist — Ami, the star of the show. Come to think of it, I want Ami, too. And while we're on the subject, I also want Chef Tom Colicchio from *Top Chef.* He's more my age, and with his bald head and intense gaze, he's my Telly Savalas.

It turns out that the power of suggestion extends to everything on TV.

Maybe I should get a tattoo of Chef Tom?

SEPTEMBER SONG

Summer's over, and I'm trying to be mature about it. I'm ignoring the depression I always feel at the end of summer and the dread at the onset of autumn. For a cheery girl, I get a little gloomy around now.

Why?

Because even though I'm allegedly grown-up, I still have the mentality of a middle-schooler: September to May sucks, and summer rocks! No more pencils, no more books! Summer is for getting crazy, and fall is for facing the music.

I don't go to school anymore, but I remain on the back-to-school mental clock. It's like I have to gear up for AP Bio, but I don't take AP Bio. I never did take AP Bio. They didn't even have AP Bio when went to high school. They had pop quizzes, and that was scary enough. "Pencils down" will forever be associated with a sick feeling in the pit of my stomach.

Nor is it as if I go back to work in September, after my summer vacation. I don't always take a vacation, and didn't this year. Like a lot of us, I work seven days a week, year round. I'm not complaining, mind you, I love my job. But it raises the question, why should I be sad that summer's over, when it's not as if it were such a big break?

The same goes for Sunday nights.

I always feel a little bummed out on Sunday nights. Sunday night is the Labor Day of the week, if you follow. It's as if the weekend = summer, and Monday = fall. This makes no sense, again, because I work on Sunday, the same as I do on Monday.

So why do I dread Monday, on Sunday night? Why do I dread fall, at the end of summer? Why do I feel this way? My days don't change one iota.

Daughter Francesca thinks she knows the answer, and she weighs in, below:

Well, Mom, that's not exactly true, your days from summer to fall do change in one respect: me. Sure, you haven't been in school in a long time, but for almost two decades, I have. For the last sixteen years, just being my mother has put you on some version of the summer vacation schedule. Although I realize that, for you, it may not

117

have always been such a vacation — driving me to day camp when I was little, watching me attempt the perfect dive for the 100th time in a day, later on, teaching me how to make the drive down to Ocean City by myself, or, most recently, giving in to my insistence that summer is the perfect time to get two kittens. For better or for worse, my summertime glee and back-to-school dread has probably rubbed off on you over the years. But that's about to change. For both of us.

In a sense, this is my last real summer. The last summer of my childhood, the last summer as a student. As I prepare to be a senior in college, I am preparing for my last academic fall. By next summer, I will be a (gulp) grown-up, or, I guess I'm supposed to say, adult. Summer vacation will shrink to two weeks, and the rest will just be going to work in hot weather. I'm excited to enter the adult world, but to be honest, I'm scared, too. I will have a new sort of weight in the pit of my stomach when I hear my last "pencils down." I'm out of time.

The chemistry test may be over, but the new test is just beginning. Is my adult life the "fall" of my summertime childhood? Now that I think about it, I don't even like the word "fall." It sounds perilous. And I'm afraid of heights.

But then again, maybe summer isn't gone for good. Of course I know the season isn't going to disappear, but I mean, summer as-I-know-it won't go away forever, either. Like you said, Mom, you still get that thrill when the spring days get longer and warmer, regardless of work schedule. It's as if the weather and the people can finally exhale into the balmy summer breeze. Summer will always be the time of short sleeves, lunch outside, and guilt-free ice cream. Last time I checked, sunshine has no age limit.

And, you know, fall isn't so bad. Fall isn't only about back-to-school. Fall is warm colors and warm houses, Thanksgiving and football, crunchy leaves and crisp air. "Fall" doesn't have to be a scary word. People fall in love. Things fall into place.

And, Mom, if what you wrote proves anything, it's that if I really miss my summer vacation, I'll always be able to relive it when I have kids of my own.

Oh wait. Now I've scared myself again.

Road Map

I write this the day after I took daughter Francesca back to college, and I miss her. I know I'm not the only sad parent. My good friend sent her son to kindergarten last week and she's still crying.

September is a time of beginnings and endings, which are not coincidentally the same thing; the beginning of middle school for your kid will finalize the ending of elementary school. Any movement your child makes toward something will be a movement away from you. And though we've all heard that dumb roots-and-wings speech, it still hurts.

You're happy for your kid, but sad for yourself.

And none of your sad feelings are supposed to show. You don't want to burden your child, especially when she's doing exactly what she's supposed to, which is growing up. So you keep the sadness inside.

Your heart says, Ouch, but your face says, Yay! It's the terrible wrench of parenting, which specializes in the bittersweet.

Oddly, I don't think we allow ourselves to acknowledge this sadness, even among us parents. I know a mother who says she feels silly because she misses her kid, away at college. We're all pretending we're too-cool-for-school, about school.

Instead, let's clarify things right now: It's okay to miss your kid. A lot.

In fact, it's essential to miss your kid a lot. If you miss your kid a lot, it's proof that you love them. That you're involved with them. That in the short time they spent in your care, you got to know them well. After all, you miss a lot of things that aren't as important, right? For example, I miss carbs.

Missing your kid is proof that you're a good parent, despite the fact that the current vogue is to put down good parents. I've seen us called the "helicopter parents," always hovering over our children, and I've read articles putting down children who remain connected to their parents by cell phone and email, calling those kids the "tethered generation."

Boy, does that burn me up.

It's good to be a helicopter parent. It's better to be a helicopter parent than to be

Britney Spears. Likewise, it's good for kids to stay connected to their parents. It's better to be a tethered kid than Lindsay Lohan.

This is why I love Brad Pitt and Angelina Jolie. They have a passel of kids and they've been married fifteen minutes. Wait, they're not married, but never mind. All I know is that in every photo I see of them, they're with their kids, doing kid things. Not only do they spend time with their kids, they *wear* their kids. They're holding at least two children at all times; one is always strapped on their front in a Snugli and the other is draped around a shoulder like a noisy handbag.

Brad and Angelina look like good parents to me. I don't sweat that they're not married. I don't think you need a marriage to raise a kid. Families come in all shapes and sizes. I became a single parent when my daughter was an infant, and I remember when someone at school told her she was an "only child." She came home and asked me, "Does that mean you're an 'only mom?' "

Answer: Yes.

I don't think it takes a village to raise a child. On the contrary, I think it takes one person who loves the child and places that child's needs and interests above his own, for a good, long time. Like decades. And if you've done that for a child, it stands to reason that you're going to miss them when they go, even if you gave them the roots and wings required by Hallmark cards.

So what do you do about this sadness you feel?

Here's how I think about it, and it helps:

Recognize that your child is just traveling through. You don't own your child. You're just her caretaker for a very long time, because you willed her into existence. Even so, her existence is separate from yours. It's easy to forget this, especially if you're a good parent, because you can get so close to your child that your interests are often perfectly aligned. You remember times when you had to fight for your child, whether it was to get her a doctor's appointment in a busy flu season or to score her the last Furby, back when every kid wanted a Furby.

But don't be fooled.

You and your child are different people, and your child is traveling through your life, just as you're traveling through hers. All of us are traveling through this life, and though our paths overlap for a time, like routes on a highway map, eventually we all separate, one from the other.

And I'm not talking about college here.

Think about traveling through, and you'll be able to let your kid go. It's just like she took the business route and you took the local. You might end up in the same place again, and it doesn't mean she won't come back, God knows.

And you can always hold the cats hostage.

American Excess

I think the world divides into two groups: people who take advantage of membership rewards programs, and people like me.

A long time ago, I applied for an American Express card, but I was rejected. I had charged my way to becoming a writer, and my credit history ranged from Slow Pay to You Must Be Joking. The measure of credit-worthiness is the FICO score, with 800 or so the best, like the old SAT scores. I couldn't get into any college on my FICO score. My FICO score was my weight.

Eventually I paid back every penny of my debts, but my FICO score haunted me. I couldn't get a credit card from Target and my books were bestsellers in Target. I don't think this happened to James Patterson.

Then, one day, American Express relented — with a qualification. They told me they would give me a "starter" American Express card. The baby Amex had a thousand-dollar credit limit and training wheels. It even looked younger; it wasn't cash-green, it was transparent, as if it couldn't be trusted with a color. It was a credit card, pre-puberty.

Still I took the card and became Financial Barbie. I never missed a payment and I sent in the whole balance every time, then I reapplied for the Big Girl American Express card. And was rejected again. But on the phone, they happened to mention that they could give me the American Express card for small business, if I were a small business. They asked, "Are you a small business?"

I answered, "Why, yes, the smallest."

On the phone, I deemed myself Lisa Scottoline, Inc., which is a new way to incorporate yourself that I invented, and they gave me a small-business credit card, which came with a higher credit limit and its own color — a respectable, corporate, gray. Since then, however, I still keep getting rejected for the real-deal American Express card.

Whatever. I've struck out three times now and I have to pretend it doesn't matter. And that's not the point, anyway.

The point is that unbeknownst to me, my small-business American Express card has, all these years, been racking up Membership Rewards.

Wow! Membership Rewards! I had no idea what that was, but it sounds great. It sounds like an exclusive club that I'm a member of, automatically. And rewards are always good. I get a reward and I didn't even find anything? Hell, I didn't even know anything was lost!

I learned about the Membership Rewards the other day, when I actually read my endless pile of junk mail. I saw a slick catalog full of mixers, Bose radios, rolling luggage, golf clubs, and "timepieces," which is what we members call watches. Instead of prices, the catalog had points. I flipped to the front and saw that I had a "point balance," which was 52,140.

Yay!

So everything in the catalog was free, or at least the stuff under 52,140 points. I was so excited that I called up my friend, but she had already spent her points on his-and-her mountain bikes, a portable DVD player, and a toaster from England. She'd even gone to Europe on her frequent flier miles, but I will never figure out how to cash in those babies and I have approximately three billion, which is twelve zillion times my SAT score and fifteen zillion times my FICO.

But I digress. I made a cup of coffee and

sat down with the Membership Rewards catalog.

Two hours later, I had dog-eared ten pages, circled fifteen items, and downed another cup of coffee. My stomach had twisted into a knot, my heart was pounding, and I was in a tizzy of indecision. I couldn't pick between the Sony digital camera, the new iPod, or the Dyson "animal vacuum," which I loved for the name.

And if I didn't want those items, the catalog offered trips, meals, and gift cards. Worse, I was even "pre-approved" for double my point balance, which admitted me to the truly pimp point class. If I wanted the awesome 37-inch plasma TV, Amex would send it to me and charge the difference — on my credit card.

Hmmm.

Bottom line, all this free stuff paralyzed me. If I had been spending dollars, I could have made the decision, but the fact that it was points had me flummoxed. I didn't want to blow my chance to get something free by getting the wrong free thing. I set the catalog aside for another day.

A point saved is a point earned.

ONE ROOM, TWO ROOM, RED ROOM, BLUE ROOM

I just got back from the White House. I stole nothing of value. More accurately, the thing I stole didn't cost anything.

Let me explain.

The National Book Festival is an annual book fair sponsored by the Library of Congress and started by First Lady Laura Bush, to promote literacy. It's held on the National Mall, where a series of tents had stages for seventy authors, representing all types of books. Approximately 150,000 people attended the Festival, a record crowd.

Reading knows no political party.

The morning of the Festival, Mrs. Bush invited the authors and their guests to the White House for a classy breakfast buffet, and we were permitted to eat anywhere we liked in the Red, Blue, and Green Rooms. My plus one was daughter Francesca, who made sure that I didn't spill coffee on the red, blue, or green rugs. I'd hate to be remembered as The One Who Assassinated the Lincoln Rug, and that wouldn't be a dry cleaning bill I'd like to pay. We're not talking a stained sweater here. We're talking a second mortgage.

So we ate our blueberry pancakes very carefully, perched on the edge of two lovely red wing chairs, and we even put an official White House napkin under our coffee cups so we didn't make a ring on the inlaid mahogany tables. But even in the White House, my home-improvement wheels got turning. People imagine what they would do if they ever got to be President, and I'm no different. For me, renovation of the White House would be the national priority.

I wouldn't hire a decorator. I'd do it myself. I'd be the Decorator-in-Chief.

We know that real estate ads are my porn, so it should come as no surprise that I have lots of great ideas about home décor, too. I'm addicted to HGTV. I memorize *House & Garden.* There's no more extreme makeover than the White House. The place has major curb appeal, and that world-leader vibe would make it the best client ever.

I smell *Architectural Digest.*

I'd start my makeover in the Red, Blue,

and Green Rooms, because they're surprisingly small and laid out in a straight line. If I were President, I'd knock down the walls and make one big family room, with space enough for a nice, built-in entertainment center. And a 70-inch plasma TV and a wet bar. Plus a computer station with 21-inch monitors. What an improvement that would be! Even the First Family needs a family room.

Obviously, I'd have to repaint the new room, too. I'd love to paint it my favorite color, which is pink, even though it's politically incorrect. It's the first thing someone would ask if a woman like me became President: "What, is she gonna paint the White House pink?"

I'd answer, "Yes. It's good to be Queen."

I'd make a few changes in the furniture department, too. The wing chairs are lovely, as are the antique tables, but you have to go with the times. You can't watch the playoffs from a wing chair. You can't rest your Diet Coke on mahogany. If I were President, I'd get me a nice, big sectional sofa. Gray ultrasuede would be chic, and I'd order it custom, with cupholders built into the armrests. That's my dream. In my Presidency, cupholders for all!

Cupholders know no political party.

And, when I looked out the bubbly glass windows of the White House, I noticed there was no attached garage. That would be a must. Also an in-ground pool, maybe next to the Rose Garden, with some tasteful fake rocks and a little waterfall, so I could listen to artificial burbling while I contemplated foreign policy or skimmed the Frontgate catalog.

In fact, I found myself wondering if the White House had a finished basement, which of course would be job one. It would make a perfect gym, and I'd fill it up with Nautilus weights and elliptical machines that I could ignore.

That's how I'd make the White House a home.

By the way, before I left the White House that day, I did get to meet the First Lady. She shook my hand and was very nice. I thanked her for the Festival, but I didn't tell her my suggestions for the house.

Or what I stole, which was the official paper napkin, embossed with the gold symbol of the President, encircled by the brown ring of my coffee cup.

You can hardly blame me for taking a memento.

Even without a Jacuzzi, it's still the White House.

CRISTOFORO

I was the Grand Marshal of the Columbus Day parade, and I liked it so much it scared me.

I walked down the street with people clapping on both sides. If I waved, they waved back. If I smiled, they smiled back. So what if they had no idea who I was? I still ate it up.

The best part was that I got to wear a sash that went sideways across my body, Miss-America style. This was a thrill for a girl who was always The Smart One. For once, I felt like The Pretty One. And let me tell you a secret: every Smart One wants to be The Pretty One.

But back to the point.

It turned out that I love a parade, especially when I'm in it. I didn't think I had a big ego, but being a Grand Anything will swell your head. By the time I got home, I could barely fit it through the front door.

I was having Delusions of Grand Marshal.

By bedtime, long after the parade had ended, my ego was only getting bigger. I tried to stuff it back into my body, but I'm only five foot two and it had inflated to the size of a bouncy house. I was full of myself, literally. I almost kept my sash on, because it looked so great with my pajamas.

Then I tried to stop thinking about me, me, me for just one moment. I reflected on the other important points of the Columbus Day parade:

That it celebrated the cultural pride and accomplishments of Italian-Americans. Those thoughts helped a little. At least I recalled that there were other people in the world, other than me. But the most important person that day wasn't any of those people, or me.

The Guest of Honor was Christopher Columbus, and my thoughts turned to him.

We learned in school that he sailed the ocean blue and discovered America, but we have learned since that he didn't find exactly what he was looking for. And of course, as they say, mistakes were made. As a result, there are people, in other cities, who picket the Columbus Day parade.

If they had picketed mine, this Grand Marshal would have given them a swift kick.

In heels.

Because Columbus wasn't alone in his mistakes. The colonization of many countries, including this one, produced some of the worst injustices in human history. We all used to think that might made right, and it's a lesson we haven't learned completely, even today.

And what is undeniable about Columbus is that he set out into uncharted territory, against all odds, risking his life to follow a dream, believing profoundly in himself, and God. Columbus's diary of his journeys, and he kept excellent notes, reveals that his crews were profoundly religious men, praying often. They were praying that Columbus was right.

They didn't want to fall off the edge of the world.

I thought about Columbus then, and about our own uncharted territory, both the good and bad. A new baby; a new diagnosis. Love is uncharted territory. So is life. We truly do not know what will happen to us tomorrow. All of it is unmapped to us, yet we sail on.

We will make mistakes.

We will be capable of great cruelty and great kindness.

We will meet those who love us and those

who don't. They might even picket our parade. Some call them haters. I call them book critics.

We might not find exactly what we were looking for.

And the odds are that we will find things that others have already found. Just this morning I discovered again how wonderful it feels to have the sun on my face. It's not a new discovery, or one as big as a continent, but it's still a thrill. And I get credit for making it. So do you.

All of our little discoveries will be new to us, and the happiness they bring can't be underestimated, nor should they be. They shouldn't go uncredited, either, nor should our efforts. On the contrary, both should be celebrated, our voyages and our discoveries.

We are all of us explorers in this life.

Christopher Columbus reminds us to sail on, to have faith, and to trust that we won't fall off.

Andiamo.

Let's go.

Hold On a Min—

Let us now praise interrupting.

I know it's an unpopular position, but I'm not one to shy away from controversy. I've already admitted to emergency-room bralessness and spitting out Dead Whoppers.

I have a habit of interrupting, and now I'm going to make a case for it.

Interrupting has gotten a bad rap for too long. Those of us who interrupt aren't being disrespectful. We're just excited by whatever it was you just said. We're so excited, in fact, that we can't wait for you to finish saying it before we respond.

You can't blame us if you're a great conversationalist.

The subject of interrupting comes up because recently I had dinner with best friend Franca. You have to trust me when I tell you that Franca is an angel. She's not only a great mother, she's a brilliant lawyer who represents children with special educational needs, and she's dedicated to her job, her clients, and their families.

But she interrupts, and so do I.

We interrupt each other all the time. You know that cliché about the friends who are so close that they finish each other's sentences?

Don't believe a word of it.

A really close friend will never finish your sentence. A close friend will interrupt your sentence and say something new. After all, you knew what you were going to say. Don't you wanna hear something else?

I could never be friends with anyone who wouldn't interrupt me. I can't imagine eating dinner with someone who sat there in stony silence while I talked. Likewise, I would never be so rude as to *not* interrupt a friend. How else would she know I was listening?

Franca and I could finish each other's sentences if we wanted to, but we don't want to. We're both so excited by what the other one just said that we can't wait to add to it, elaborate on it, or give another example. Plus, we know that the end of each other's sentences isn't always necessary. In our sentences, we get to the point right away, and the rest is usually repetition.

So the other night when we had dinner,

we interrupted each other constantly through the appetizer, and by the entrée, we were interrupting each other so seamlessly that we were both talking nonstop at the exact same time. What a great conversation!

We weren't offended. We were excited!

If you're not buying my excited argument, try this one: it saves a lot of time to have two conversations at once. Interrupting is multitasking, only with words. That night, if Franca and I had conversed in the mundane, conventional, taking-turns-in-preschool way, we'd still be at the restaurant.

Interrupting is efficient.

Interrupting saves energy.

Interrupting is green!

And when I looked around the restaurant that night, I much preferred our table to the others. At those tables, there were couples, but none of them was talking. I gather this would be the height of good manners, with nobody interrupting anybody.

There was even a table with a couple who wasn't talking, and between them sat their toddler, who was watching Winnie The Pooh on a portable DVD player. I guess they brought the video so their child wouldn't interrupt their not interrupting each other. The only one talking at that table was Tigger, who was interrupting Pooh.

Tigger's excited!

And help me out here, but don't you think that your opinion on interrupting depends on whether you run on estrogen or testosterone?

Case in point. I didn't even realize that anyone thought interrupting was rude until my second marriage. Thing Two did not like to be interrupted. One day, he said to me, "Will you ever stop interrupting me?"

I answered, "Why?"

So you can see how it didn't work out.

And in my experience in aggravating people, I've noticed that women are never aggravated when you interrupt them, and men always are, based on my sample of Thing Two and a couple of testy dates, which I admit might be statistically slim.

The exception is Chris Matthews.

I love Chris Matthews. I should have married Chris Matthews. Chris Matthews interrupts all the time and doesn't even apologize. On the contrary, the whole point of his TV show is interrupting, which he has redefined as a sign of intelligent conversation. This was a genius move by a guy who just likes to interrupt. It's not rude, it's

Hardball.

It's the boy version of *Excited!*

Compare and contrast with *The View,* a TV show in which four women are always interrupting each other. It's not seen as intelligent conversation, it's seen as a hen party.

So please, discuss among yourselves the issue of interrupting.

And remember, show your excitement!

THANKSGIVING

Thanksgiving is about family, so I thought I'd ask daughter Francesca for her thoughts about the day. We spend so much time talking to and teaching our children that sometimes it's nice just to ask them what they think, and listen to the answer. So take a minute this Thanksgiving to ask your own baby birds what they think about the day, and listen to whatever they chirp up with.

Because I bet that the thing that you're most thankful for is them.

From Francesca:

My family is small. Since it's only my mom and me at home, our Thanksgiving has never been the Martha Stewart production it can be for some other families. My dad's family has Thanksgiving in New York; my grandmother and uncle have Thanksgiving in Miami. My mother and I buy a last-minute turkey, make up some wacky ingredients for a stuffing, and eat together with Frank Sinatra playing in the background and a lot of warm, furry dogs warming our feet. It has always been nice, and I know we're lucky to have each other, but sometimes it has just felt small.

Until Harry.

Harry is our neighbor, he's in his eighties, and we got to know him from running into him when we walked our dogs. He used to go for a long walk every day, waving a white handkerchief so cars would see him. He would stop to chat with us, always cheery and warm, even when the late-autumn wind made his nose red and his eyes tear.

A few years ago, my mom invited Harry to our Thanksgiving dinner, and he arrived at four o'clock sharp, wearing a cozy, Icelandic sweater and graciously removing his Irish tweed cap as soon as he came inside. During dinner, my mom asked him about his hobbies, and to be honest, I didn't expect this to be the most thrilling conversation topic. After all, my grandmother's hobbies are crosswords and yelling at my uncle. But Harry's face lit up at the question.

"I'm a Ham!" he said.

We didn't get it.

And with that, Harry turned into a livewire. He talked about his hobby as a Ham

Radio operator, a mode of amateur radio broadcast first popular in the 1920s. Harry told us all about using radio technology while serving in WWII, and we sat, rapt, as he described sending a signal into the air, bouncing it off the stratosphere, and bending it around the earth. He seemed like Merlin, hands waving in the air — his fingers had lost their quiver and his watery eyes were bright and shining.

Well-meaning, but being somewhat of a teenage buzz kill, I asked, "Have you ever tried email? Wouldn't that be easier?"

No, he said. He enjoys the effort — a foreign concept in my wireless Internet, instant-messaging world. Even though ham radios can communicate through voice, he still uses Morse code sometimes, just for the fun of it. Most of all, he enjoys belonging to the community of Hams. "I get to meet people I would never meet. I have friends around the world."

That night, it didn't matter that Harry and I didn't share a last name, or that we didn't share the same relatives or the same nose. That Thanksgiving, he was family. He still is.

What Harry and my mother taught me that Thanksgiving, whether they knew it or not, was that you don't just get your family, you can create your family. We do it all the time without realizing it; we form bonds with the people we work with, live with, learn with. I've felt homesick up at college, but I've also created my own little family of friends at school. I hope all those brave soldiers overseas have found second families in their comrades, people to support and lean on when they're forced to be away from loved ones at home.

These second families don't replace our first one, they just extend it.

It wasn't until that Thanksgiving with Harry that I really got it: there are no rules for what or who makes a family, no limit on love. The holidays especially are a time when we can reach out and say "thank you" to all the people who make up our many families. And sometimes, if you're lucky like me, Thanksgiving can even be a chance to set an extra plate at the table.

Looking out the dining room window, I can barely see Harry's house for the trees. But inside that house is a man who is not alone. There lives a man who is an expert at reaching out to people, whether by angling radio waves around the globe, or by flagging us down on a walk around the block. He has us, he has our other neighbors, he has friends around the world. Even better,

we have him.
  And for that, I am thankful.

PRICELESS

I'm going to tell you the secret behind successful holiday shopping. And it's contrary to everything you have learned.

They tell you that when you're giving a gift, you should give the other person what they like, not what you like. Well, that credo is exactly, one hundred percent, wrong.

I used to do my holiday shopping just that way. I'd pass up beautiful stuff that any sane person would love and I'd waste good money on stupid junk. The rationale was that if they were happy, I was happy.

But I wasn't.

I recognized this credo as codependency in disguise. I was enabling bad taste and bad judgment. Now, I am codependent no more. If they want Big Mouth Billy Bass, they have to buy it themselves.

And worse, I used to ask people what they wanted, which was the biggest no-no ever. Every Christmas, I would ask my mother, and she would tell me. Problem was, everything my mother wanted was impossible to find.

One year, she wanted a knit poncho. Another year, a nightgown with no elastic at the wrists. A third, a perfume she remembered from World War II, called Pois De Senteur, which I think translates to Peas of Health. I gave up after six stores and bought her a bottle of Joy. Her Christmas was joyless.

Then I wised up.

I stopped asking her what she wanted and started getting her what I wanted. And the ironic part is, I learned this from my mother herself.

My mother never gave me what I wanted for Christmas, but gave me only what she wanted. For example, when I was in middle and high school, she fell in love with what she called "estate jewelry." To this day, I have no idea what "estate jewelry" really means. I don't think she did, either. I bet she liked the "estate" part, which sounds classy. If you put "estate" together with "jewelry," you get a mental image of glittery people in tuxes, swanning around mansions. But in truth, I suspect that the term refers to jewelry left by someone who has died, which nobody in her family wanted, even though it was free.

Do you understand the significance of this?

In other words, even if her family loved this woman, they didn't want that jewelry, which should give you an excellent idea of what estate jewelry looks like, or, at least, the estate jewelry that my mother picked out for me. She gave me a bronze brooch shaped like a spiked sun. A snake bracelet, complete with scales and a forked tongue, that curled around my upper arm. A pendant with a blue ceramic eye in the center.

The kind of junk that turned my jewelry chest into Pandora's box.

Back then, my mother gave me estate jewelry like it was going out of style, which it was, by definition. Undoubtedly, it cost way too much of her secretary's salary, so I opened my presents from her with a guilty and sinking heart. On the bright side, I had the best brooch collection of any thirteen-year-old, ever.

I know I sound like a terrible person, whining about this, but here's the point, about why you should buy people what you want:

Because now, over time, my thinking has changed, and so has my taste in many things. Today I look at the jewelry she gave me through the lens of perspective and maturity. Do I still find it unbelievably ugly?

Of course.

I would sooner go braless in the emergency room than wear one of those brooches, and we both know how I feel about emergency-room bralessness.

But nevertheless, now I treasure each one of these pieces of jewelry. Each one of them has enormous sentimental value to me. Each one reminds me that my mother spent money on me that she didn't have. Each one tells me how much she loves me. Each is the best present I could have gotten, for that holiday or any holiday.

And why?

Because my mother gave me things that she loved. So when I look at all that awful stuff, I see what I love the most.

Her.

HOLIDAY GUILT

We all have so much to do around the holidays, and it can be hard to prioritize. But I have a secret weapon that you might like, too, so I'll fill you in:

My secret weapon is guilt.

I no longer try to free myself from guilt. Instead, I welcome guilt and put it to work for me. I built myself a Guilt-O-Meter with a 1–10 scale, which I consult whenever a task presents itself. If it's a task I'd feel too guilty to ignore, the needle on the Guilt-O-Meter goes to 10, and I do it right away. For example, work scores a 10 on the Guilt-O-Meter, so I work a lot. This is good for my mortgage payments, if not my social life, but whatever. Life is too short to live with guilt. I say, do what your guilt tells you.

Right now.

On my Guilt-O-Meter, all housework scores between 1 and 3, except for ironing or cleaning my closet, which are both 0.

Recycling is a 10, but rinsing the bottles first is a 2. Working out is supposed to be a 9, but it's secretly a 5. Accumulating late fees at the library is a 7, but at the Block-buster, it's a 2. Why? The former is guilt-inducing, and the latter merely annoying. This isn't about the Merely Annoying-O-Meter.

Of course, you don't have to agree with my scores. Use them as guilt guidelines. Feel free to customize your Guilt-O-Meter.

Pimp your guilt!

My Guilt-O-Meter malfunctions during the holidays because there are too many tasks for its sensitive needle. There's no guilt like Christmas Guilt. Just ask Ebenezer Scrooge. And it's not only Christmas Guilt. I grew up in a Jewish neighborhood, and when my friends told me they got Hanuk-kah gelt, I thought they said Hanukkah guilt. Now I have Hanukkah Guilt, too.

During the holidays, my Work Guilt con-flicts with so many other guilt options. Not-Sending-Out-Greeting-Cards Guilt is a 6. Cat-Hair-in-Scotch-Tape Guilt is a 5. However, Gift-Wrap-Without-Ribbon Guilt is a 0.

Let go of the ribbon thing, people. We can only do so much.

My Guilt-O-Meter failed me recently, and

it was all because of the holidays. One morning, I woke up in a paroxysm of Gift Guilt because I hadn't bought a single present yet. A paroxysm is off the Guilt-O-Meter, scoring a 283,949. Paroxysms are usually reserved for Forgetting-Your-Mother's-Birthday Guilt, which I don't have, or Accidentally-Cutting-Your-Dog's-Ear-When-You-Clipped-Her-Fur Guilt, which I do.

Anyway, when I woke up in the paroxysm, I knew I had to get to the mall immediately. I hurried to the bathroom, where I noticed that the toilet flushed too slowly. I needed to get it checked, but calling a plumber scored only a 1 on the Guilt-O-Meter. I made a mental note to call him later, then clean my closet and iron something.

I dressed, hurried downstairs, and got a drink of water. Oddly, the garbage disposal was backing up, so I took another Guilt-O-Meter reading. A broken garbage disposal rated only another 1. I figured I'd call the disposal guy after I called the plumber after I cleaned my closet and ironed something.

So I went to the mall, shopped all day, and bought so many presents that my Gift Guilt fell to 0. My Credit Card Guilt up-ticked to 3, but that's comfortable for me. I left the mall happy, or in any event, much less guilty.

But when I got home, there was bad news. I'll try not to be disgusting, so I'll just say that the toilet had exploded and my first floor hallway was awash in human waste. I called the plumber and told him what happened, and he asked:

"Is it an emergency?"

Hmmm. I knew why he asked that. Because he was taking a Guilt-O-Meter reading of his own, and Exploding-Toilet-on-a-Friday-Night Guilt was only a 2. Especially when it was Somebody-Else's-Toilet-Around-the-Holidays Guilt.

I bet I reached him at the mall.

For a crazy minute I was stricken with Asking-For-Help Guilt. My Guilt-O-Meter needle shot up to 8, and the wimp inside me said, "Lisa, you meanie, you're asking him to work on the weekend."

Then I flipped it.

I work on the weekend, so why shouldn't the plumber? Work = 10. His Guilt-O-Meter was clearly on the fritz. Anyway, I was pretty sure that if you looked up emergency in the dictionary, you'd see a picture of my first floor hallway.

I told the plumber, "You're darn tootin' it's an emergency, buddy." Then I put on my galoshes, grabbed the Clorox and a mop, and started cleaning.

So take a lesson from me. This holiday season, let your guilt be your guide.

Except when it comes to plumbing.

THANK YOU

Lots of people travel around the holidays, and I'm no exception. I've been driving around like crazy, and if I'm driving, that means I'm getting lost.

Luckily, my car isn't.

I have one of those navigation systems, so my car knows where it is at all times. Yesterday, when I missed the turn for I-95 and found myself in Saddle River, New Jersey, it told me to take two left turns and a right, which set me instantly back on track. It even located me near the rest stop, so I could go to the bathroom. I think it knew I had to go to the bathroom.

In fact, it's so smart it could probably go to the bathroom for me.

Not only that, if I press a button, my navigation system will tell me where all the other rest stops are in New Jersey, so I have a complete array of rest stop options. After all, I may be feeling more Joyce Kilmer than

Vince Lombardi.

I love my navigation system very deeply. It's always there for me, wherever I am. It asks nothing of me, but does its job competently and professionally. It even has a cute little accent, of indeterminate origin. And though it's always right, it never says I-told-you-so.

If I could marry my navigation system, I would.

I would even vow to love, honor, and obey it. Because the only times I've gone wrong are when I haven't obeyed my navigation system. In fact, my navigation system is the only thing in the world I will ever obey.

I feel almost as good about my cell phone. The other day I realized that I had forgotten the date of a doctor's appointment, but I didn't have the doctor's phone number to call them and ask. I called 411, but they didn't have the number either, for some reason.

Luckily, my cell phone is smarter than I am.

It remembered that I had called the doctor once before and it kept the number, even though I didn't. So I called the doctor and found out that I had missed my appointment.

If my cell phone had had the appointment,

it would have been there.

And now there are cell phones that not only remember your doctor's number, but even have a navigation system. Those cell phones are going to take over the world. I advise you to get one, before it gets you.

My TV is a brainiac, too. I was watching it when all of a sudden a little sign came on the screen, reminding me that I had wanted to record a show that was playing on another channel. Of course, I had totally forgotten that I wanted to record the show, but my TV remembered. Unfortunately, it couldn't remind me why I had wanted to record such a dumb show. But that may be too much to ask of a TV.

Until next year.

Then, our TVs will record shows that we meant to record, but forgot to. And shows that we didn't want to record, but should have. And shows that they don't even make, but they should. Like funny ones.

The other day, I got to thinking about how lucky we are to live in a country in which we are so well taken care of. Our navigation systems, cell phones, and televisions are working hard for us, when we aren't. They have our lives in hand, so we aren't bothered. They ask nothing in return. They don't even resent us when we don't say thank you.

They free us to do what we want to do.

They give us peace of mind.

This holiday, we'll all be giving gifts like crazy, tons of navigation systems, cell phones, and TVs. I'm going to be giving them, too, so my family and friends will always be able to see whatever dumb show they want to see. So they'll be able to talk to whomever they want to talk to, and say what they want to say. And so that no matter where they go, whenever they get lost, they can always find their way back home.

And this holiday, when I give gifts to the people I love, I won't forget for a minute the people serving so far away in Iraq, Afghanistan, and all around the world, who are giving all of us the gift of their very selves.

They do not ask to be thanked, but that doesn't mean they don't deserve to be thanked. They are paying for our gifts with something far more precious than money.

Thank you, soldiers everywhere, this holiday.

We love and appreciate you.

May you find your way home soon.

UNRESOLUTIONS

This is the time of year when people make New Year's resolutions, but I have a better idea. By definition, a resolution is something you want to change about yourself, something you've done wrong in the past that you want to start doing right.

Boo!

I think we would all be better served if this New Year, we made unresolutions. That is, let's make a list of things we've been doing and we'd like to keep doing.

Who needs negativism around the holidays? Times are tough, and why should we make them tougher? Especially on our favorite people in the world, namely ourselves.

Let's give it a try, shall we?

I'll go first.

UnResolution Number One. I sleep in my clothes, and I resolve to keep sleeping in my clothes. I know this sounds weird, and it helps that my clothes are fleece pants and a fleece top, because I work at home. Sometimes I even wear a fleece hat to bed, like a nightcap, because I like my room cold but not my head. Bottom line, I never have to worry about what to wear, and I'm already dressed, all the time. So now you know.

UnResolution Number Two. I kiss my pets on the lips, and I like it. I know people say it's unsanitary, but they're no fun. All of my animals expect me to kiss them on the lips, even my pony. And if they balk, I grab them by their furry cheeks and force them to stand still. I'm paying the room and board, and all I want is a little smooch. Ain't nothing wrong with that.

UnResolution Number Three. I don't own an iron. It's not the worst thing in the world if my clothes are a little wrinkly. No one really notices, or if they do, they're too polite to say so, which is the same thing. To me.

UnResolution Number Four. I talk to strangers. I get this from Mother Mary, who, when we went into the Acme, talked to the produce guy, the stock boy, and the cashier. She was always up in their business, and in time, they were up in hers. It turned every errand into a little party, a reunion of old friends, but there just happens to be a cash register in the middle.

UnResolution Number Five. I make too much food. If I serve dinner and no one at the table says, "You made too much food," then I feel like I failed. I love the idea that there's a lot of food on the table. I want everybody full and happy, and I always give the leftovers to the dogs and cats. You know what comes next. (I kiss them on the lips.)

UnResolution Number Six. I wear flats. I used to always wear high heels, because I'm a shorty. I thought I felt more powerful in heels, but all I really felt was more painful. It was daughter Francesca who got me started wearing flats, and it changed my life. My toes are always happy, and I'm still a mighty mite.

UnResolution Number Seven. I buy too many books. I love to read and have hundreds of books overflowing my bookshelves and stacked high on my dining room table, in piles. I love living around books, and reading is like traveling without baggage claim. Who needs a dining room anyway?

So maybe now you understand why I'm single.

Which brings me to UnResolution Number Eight. I live alone, but I'm not lonely. I know lots of you live alone, whether by choice or by circumstance, and you may be lonely, especially around the holidays. I'm not saying you're not allowed to be, all I'm saying is that the fact that you live alone doesn't necessarily mean you're lonely. It means you're free to wear hats to bed.

In the end, our own personal happiness is about figuring out what makes us feel the most ourselves, and living that way — and to hell with what anybody else thinks.

So when you're making a list of resolutions, please do make some unresolutions, too.

It will be a Happier New Year.

HEARING VOICES

We've all heard that when you have to make a decision, you should listen to your inner voice.

But I have a question.

What if you disagree with your inner voice?

For example, here's what happened to me. I went to Boston to see daughter Francesca in a show that ran for three weekends. I decided to stay for the duration because it was easier than driving back and forth, and happily for me, as a writer, I can work anywhere.

Especially where there's room service.

I write great whenever room service is around. I love room service like Hemingway loved Scotch. I think the course of American letters would have been completely different if Fitzgerald had known about In-Room Dining. I bet Faulkner would have gone with the mustard salmon with *pommes frites*.

He might have written *As I Lay Eating,* instead.

Anyway, I stayed in a hotel and even brought my dog Ruby, who once killed my finger. If I left her at home, I was afraid she'd kill something else, namely one of the other dogs. Besides, it's fun to have a dog in a hotel.

She likes room service, too.

For the last weekend of the show, mother and brother flew up from Miami and we had a great time. Afterwards, we were scheduled to drive home together on Sunday, but when we woke up that morning, it was snowing like crazy. Almost a foot of snow had already fallen, and freezing rain, hail, and other pointy things poured from the sky. Only snow plows, salt trucks, and the proverbial emergency vehicles were on the roads. The governor issued the usual travel advisory, which boiled down to:

Are you nuts?

So mother, brother, daughter, and I convened in a hotel room to make a decision about whether to stay or go. Mother said, "It's cockamamie to drive in this weather."

Brother said, "Let's stay an extra day and go home Monday."

Daughter said, "I vote for Monday, too."

My inner voice agreed with all of them. It

said, It's only common sense to stay another day. Plus, I can order that roast chicken I like. They'd cook it for me and bring it on a tray with a rose, then take away the dirty dishes, like I'm a baby. A little writer baby.

But I disagreed with my inner voice. A contrary voice was coming out of me, and I think it was my outer voice. It said, I've been in this hotel for almost three weeks. It's costing me a fortune. I finished my book. I'm out of underwear and Iams. I want to go home, and the governor is not the boss of me.

So I said, "I have four-wheel drive. Let's rock."

We left at noon in a blizzard, and we were the only car on the Massachusetts Turnpike. At least I think we were, but I couldn't see much through the sleet frozen on the windshield, in patches shaped like major continents. I couldn't clear the windshield because ice clung to the wipers, transforming them into twin Popsicles. I blasted the defrost on MAX, but the effect was MIN, except that windows steamed up and the interior temperature hovered at greenhouse effect.

I couldn't drive above 45 mph because once I hit 50, we fishtailed, which was when I realized that although I had a will in place, all of my beneficiaries were in the car. So if we all died driving home, my hard-earned money would go to the state, in which case the governor would be the boss of me.

We stopped four times on the way, both for dogs and people, and the lowest moment occurred at a "canteen" in Connecticut, when we got out and saw that the car was completely encased in a thin layer of ice, as if it had grown an impervious shell, like the Batmobile.

That is, if the Batmobile contained The Flying Scottolines and a corgi with behavioral problems.

We finally got home at nine o'clock that night. Bottom line, a trip that usually took six hours took three extra. And the whole way, I was hearing voices. It was my Inner Voice yelling at my Outer Voice.

But amazingly, when we got home, neither mother, brother, daughter, or dog said I-told-you-so.

Which is why they're the beneficiaries.

WHOOPEE SOCKS

Mother Mary is visiting, and you know what that means. More Scottoline family hijinks, most recently in the clothes department. The change in climate from Miami to Philly has caused major wardrobe drama, and at all times, we have much discussion about what my mother should wear that day. Turtlenecks strangle her. Wool scratches her. Silk snags. Acrylic is perfect but only in cardigans. Layers are too bunchy. Given how picky my mother is, imagine my surprise when she came down for breakfast one morning wearing a white lab coat over her clothes.

My daughter and I exchanged glances. Mind you, Mother Mary is 4'11" tall and about a hundred pounds. Her hair is white and cut close to her head, and with her brown eyes behind round glasses and her nose curved like a beak, she looks like a baby snow owl. But in the lab coat, she could have been Dr. Bunsen Honeydew from *The Muppet Show.*

Why she was wearing a lab coat, I had no idea. I didn't even know she had gone to medical school.

"Ma, is the doctor in?" I asked, setting a mug of coffee in front of her.

"What do you mean?"

"Why are you wearing a lab coat?"

"I'm eighty-three. Can't I wear what I want?"

"But where'd you get a lab coat?"

"What's the difference?"

"I'm just curious. Don't you think it's a little strange?"

"Why?"

I gave up. Answering a question with a question is my mother's favorite thing, and if she wanted to play Dr. Mom, it was fine with me. Plus I had noticed that some older people get tired of dressing normal and start wearing strange outfits. Not all older people, but some. I'm not naming names. They've been getting dressed nice for a long time, and at some point, some of them they just stop bothering. For example, under her lab coat, my mother had on cotton pants and a Miami Vice T-shirt she's worn since Don Johnson was hot.

Who can blame her?

Not me, not really.

At her age, I'll probably be the same way. In fact, I'm the same way already. When I'm in first-draft hibernation, I wear the same fisherman's sweater every day, which I bought for twenty dollars from a street vendor in New York. It smells like the subway and guarantees I'll be single forever. It's the comfort food of clothes, and since it harms no one, who cares?

I started frying eggs when daughter Francesca said, "I like the lab coat. Wouldn't it be funny if we all wore uniforms instead of clothes?"

"It might." I decided to play along. "What uniform would you wear?"

"A trashman jumpsuit."

"Why?"

"It would be so easy, and if you got trash on it, it wouldn't matter."

My mother nodded. "See, that's why I like my white coat. It's so easy."

Wrong. Chico's is easy. Lab coats are crazy.

It got me thinking about uniforms. I remembered with fondness my sash from the Columbus Day parade, but that's not the same thing. A mail lady uniform would be cool, because you can carry dog biscuits in the big pockets. The UPS guy gets to wear knee socks, which are way easier than

pantyhose, but who wears pantyhose anyway? I wouldn't mind a chef's uniform,
because I could gain three hundred pounds
and still fit into those checkered pants.

Then I knew. "I'd go with a motorcycle
cop uniform. I like the boots."

"And the gun," my mother added.

Francesca looked over.

Half the time, we get in a wardrobe rut
that might as well be a uniform, right? For
example, when I'm in second draft, which
lasts three months, I switch to the sweater-
jeans-Danskos trifecta common to suburban
moms and English majors. At book signings, I pair a pretentious jacket with pretentious jeans, because they match. And the
little black dress is my uniform for the night
shift.

Maybe it's not the worst thing. Uniforms
make our life easy. What we wear reflects
the way we see ourselves and sends a clear
message about us.

My mother was saying, "My sister had
quite an outfit. After she lost all that weight,
she used to go down the Navy Yard in shorts
and high heels, with whoopee socks."

"What are whoopee socks?" my daughter
asked, and my mother lifted a thin, white
eyebrow.

"You know."

But maybe not all messages need to be so clear.

Wants and Needs

Daughter Francesca came home from visiting a friend the other day and said, "Mom, you know what you need?"

Uh oh.

Leave it to your kids to let you know what you need. You thought you had what you needed, if not everything you wanted, and you were happy with that, because you adhere to the teachings of a certain philosopher-king who says that you can't always get what you want, but you can get what you need.

"What do we need?" I asked.

"A home theater."

"Do tell."

So Francesca sat down at the kitchen island and told me all about her friend's home theater. A plush room with a huge-screen TV. Picture quality to rival any multiplex. Three stepped rows of cushy recliners that moved forward and back at the touch of a button. Stereo speakers for crystal-clear digital sound. No windows or noise to cause glare or distraction. In short, a total movie experience, without the long lines, sticky floors, or suspect upholstery.

By the end of the conversation, you know what I was thinking. Mick Jagger is a false idol, and I need a home theater.

All I have is a home, and while I used to think that was enough, I was wrong.

My new home theater was already taking shape in my mind, fully-loaded. It included all of the above, plus some custom touches that Francesca and I came up with. Cup-holders in the recliners. A popcorn machine. We stopped short of the mannequin inside the fake ticket window, because that would be creepy.

We even thought of signs we could hang on the walls: There's no place like home theater. Bless this home theater. Home, sweet, home theater.

Then we started walking around our house, figuring out which room we could destroy, I mean, convert.

We considered the family room, but it had too many pesky windows, and even if we put up shades, we could never get the room dark enough. There was just too much sunlight streaming in, ruining everything.

Plus views of evergreen trees and holly bushes we'd have to obliterate.

We considered the basement, but I nixed that idea. My basement is dark enough, but it's cold and damp. Spiders live there, and the occasional mouse.

All my mice are occasional.

If they weren't, that would be a problem I'd have to do something about and the kind of thing you'd never admit to in print. I know they're occasional because I put occasional traps down and find dead mice, but only on occasion. Also I think of them as field mice, which are a normal and natural part of country life, and not mere rodents, which are disgusting. And I do live in a rural area, if you don't count the Corporate Center. So all I have, really, are occasional field mice.

Either way, the basement home theater isn't happening.

Unless the movie is *Willard.*

We went to the dining room and looked it over. I have a symbolic dining room and consider myself lucky. In my broke days, I always dreamed of having a house with a dining room I didn't use. It's not as if my dining room is too fancy to use, because nothing in my house is too fancy. It's that I've run out of bookshelves, so books cover all the surfaces in the dining room, including the table and chairs. While some people have a pile of books to be read, the so-called TBR pile, I have a dining roomful of books to be read, or a TBR dining room. The books present an obstacle to a home theater, but I can't bring myself to replace Thoreau with *Transformers III.*

So the dining room is out.

We ran out of rooms and looked around for a place to build an addition for the home theater, but by then we both knew we were pipe dreaming. There was no place for an addition, and it would cost a fortune. We resigned ourselves to the fact that our home would forever lack a home theater.

But we hold out hope that those friends of hers will ask us over.

Charity begins at home theater.

MEOW

So I have two kittens, Mimi and Vivi. They're eight months old and although they look a lot alike, their personalities couldn't be more different.

This is A Tale of Two Kitties.

Mimi is an adorable black-and-white kitten who looks like Figaro from Disney's *Pinocchio,* with white paws like cartoon gloves and a matching stripe down the center of her face. She has golden eyes set close together, and her nose is jet black. She loves to be petted, eats whatever is put in front of her, and wakes me up by dancing on my face.

She also has a repertoire of great noises, including a gratifying purr and a questioning chirp that sounds like, Mrrrp? And when she chirps, she curls her black tail into a question mark. Genius.

If Mimi catches a mouse, she brings it to me alive, so that I can scoop the poor thing into a tumbler and set it free. Obviously, she doesn't have the heart to kill anything.

In fact, Mimi is so affectionate that the other day, my daughter came hurrying into the kitchen to say that she had been petting the kitten, who had actually drooled with happiness. I didn't believe it, so Francesca returned Mimi to her lap and scratched the kitten's head. In a few minutes, Mimi drifted into a feline fugue state and started dripping.

It was cuter than it sounds.

Our other kitten, Vivi, is also adorable. She looks remarkably like Mimi, but is gray where Mimi is black. An upside-down V on Vivi's forehead reminds me of a demented Harry Potter, and her eyes are the green of martini olives. She has a perfect slate nose and delicate ears.

But beauty is only fur deep.

If Mimi is Gallant, Vivi is Ted Bundy.

Last week, Vivi killed three mice, two moles, and a large dove. She also killed three more snakes in addition to the one she exterminated when she was only two months old. And yesterday she came home with fresh blood on her fur.

I think she buried the body.

Unlike sunny Mimi, Vivi has a dark side. It's like a Patty Duke episode, but one of the Patty Dukes is homicidal.

They say that serial killers start with killing animals. So what do animal serial killers start with? It's a good question.

Vivi knows the answer.

When she's not killing things, Vivi spends her day ignoring me. Whenever I try to pet her, she runs away. She hates to be picked up. She never purrs. Not only doesn't she love me, she doesn't like me. In fact, she doesn't even recognize me. Every time I come home, she cocks her head as if to say, Have we met?

But that's not my point.

My point is, why did one kitten turn out so good, and the other not-so-good? I am the mother of an only child, so I have no experience with raising two of anything. I treated the kittens exactly the same, yet they turned out completely different.

Where did I go wrong?

I can't figure it out. I love both kittens equally. I haven't shown any favoritism. Yet Mimi adores me, and Vivi wishes me dead.

And you, too.

Bribes don't work. I offer them Flaked Chicken & Tuna Feast, plus all manner of fish-shaped oily treats, to the same result. Mimi gobbles them up, but Vivi turns away. I even bought them both the same toy bird on a string, which Mimi happily batted, cute as an illustration in a children's book. But Vivi only watched from the sidelines. If the bird was dead, the fun was over.

I even got them catnip, which Mimi rolled around in, purring. Vivi merely left the room. She has outgrown gateway drugs. As we speak, she's probably out dealing.

Things got worse when Vivi came home with a cut on her ear, from a brawl outside with God-knows-what. A hawk, or maybe a dragon. So I took her to the vet, and he told me I had to give her an antibiotic with a medicine dropper.

Are you kidding, doc?

Vivi won't let me hold her, much less stick something in her mouth. So I put on a down coat and leather gloves to dose her, and still she raged like Charlize Theron in *Monster.*

One way or the other, the fact that Vivi turned out so bad will get blamed on me. People always blame the mother, and it's not fair. Look at Mrs. Spears, Britney's mother. Sure, she raised Britney, but her other daughter turned out . . . oh, wait. Okay, never mind. Maybe Mrs. Spears gave them too much wet food?

Nevertheless, I have to admit that I still love Vivi. I keep hoping I can turn her around. Gain her trust. Win her love. Maybe I've been too much of a friend, and not enough of a parent.

It might take a new bribe. I haven't tried the Gourmet Gold Filet Mignon Flavor with Real Seafood & Shrimp. That's even better than the food at my last wedding.

No matter, I'll never give up on Vivi.

Even a bad girl needs love.

MYSTERIES OF LIFE,
PART UNO

There's a lot of talk lately about the big mysteries of life. By that phrase, people seem to mean how the Earth began or other questions that only public television can answer.

Honestly, I'm more interested in the small mysteries of life. The mysteries that stump us day-to-day. The mysteries we need to figure out to make our lives better.

Like magazine renewals.

I'm a big fan of magazines. Actually I'm a big fan of reading anything, including cereal boxes, which is why I knew the word "riboflavin" at an early age. But when I grew up, I loved magazines like *Seventeen.* The day they publish a magazine called *Fifty-Two,* I'm in.

I subscribe to a bunch of magazines; *People, Us Weekly, Time, The New Yorker, House & Garden, Vogue, Publishers Weekly,* and *Cosmopolitan. Cosmo* is for my daughter. I'm no longer qualified to teach her about sex, since I forget.

To stay on point, I love all these magazines, and because I love them so much, I try to avoid the dreaded Interruption in Service. In my broke days, I had one of those with the electric company, and it was no fun at all. I prefer to keep my magazines up and running, with their current flowing smoothly.

But the mystery is that I can never figure out when to renew, mainly because the magazines send me so many renewal forms, almost as soon as my subscription has begun. *Time* magazine sends renewal forms even before you get your first issue of *Time,* or maybe whenever you use the word *time,* or even if you wonder what time it is. You read their magazine, but they read your mind.

There's simply no other explanation for their speed. If I ever have a heart attack, give my nitro to *Time* magazine.

And the subscription rates are a mystery, too. All the forms offer special rates. Some have a special rate if you subscribe for two or more years, others if you want to buy a gift subscription, and still others if you like the color blue. I get the distinct impression that special rates aren't all that special in magazine-land.

As Gilbert & Sullivan say, If everybody's somebody, then nobody's anybody.

And then there are the offers for a professional rate, which I'm offered all the time. The magazines seem to think that I'm a professional, and as flattered as I am, I have to wonder. How do they know what I do and whether I'm professional at it? Plus, what type of professional do you have to be to get a professional rate for *Cosmo*?

Don't answer.

For a while, I thought I was onto their game, and so I ignored the snowglobe of renewal offers. I figured I would renew when I sensed my subscription was about to expire. Wait them out. Play renewal chicken.

But I lost.

I got so used to ignoring renewal forms, I must've ignored the wrong 300 of them, because now I have an Interruption in Service in both *People* and *Time* magazines. I don't know about you, but I need *People* magazine. I pounce on it the moment it comes in and gobble it right up. I also need *Time* magazine, so I can put it on my coffee table and impress people.

Ironically, *People* doesn't impress people.

So I renewed *People* and *Time,* and determined not to ignore any more renewal forms. I figured they must know better than I do when my subscription expires. So I responded to the various offers for special professionals like me, but I still messed up. Now I get two copies of *Us Weekly* every week, which is four times as much Lindsay Lohan as I can take. (Although I do love *Us Weekly*'s feature, They're Just Like Us, which shows celebrities on their continuous vacations, proving conclusively that They're Not Like Us At All.)

On top of my double dose of *Us Weekly*, somehow I started getting *Rolling Stone*, to which I never subscribed. I have no idea how this happened. I like *Rolling Stone*, though I have no business getting it. I stopped rolling a long time ago. Nowadays, I'm happy just to sit and stay. I'm more a rock than a stone, these days.

But it's a mystery why *Rolling Stone* started coming to me. I'm guessing that my magazines know a renewal rookie when they see one and they passed the word.

It's a mystery of life, to me. I'm a mystery writer, and even I'm stumped.

Maybe I need to be a mystery of life writer.

TIME TRAVELS

Mother Mary has gone back to Miami, and I miss her snowy white hair, her homemade meatballs, and her lab coat. And there's one other thing I miss.

Her back scratcher.

Yes, you read it right. She has a back scratcher, which she brought to my house with her. Of course, like any smart-alecky daughter, I gave her a lot of grief when I saw it, as she was unpacking.

"Who travels with a back scratcher?" I asked.

"Who doesn't?" she answered, because, as you may remember, Mother Mary always answers a question with a question.

So I let it go. Mother has had a back scratcher for as long as I can remember. I'm not sure if this is an age thing or a Mary Scottoline thing. I don't know anyone else who owns a back scratcher, much less who won't leave home without one. The back scratcher she had when I was little was of pink plastic, with a tiny hand at the end. It looked like a baby arm.

Borderline creepy.

Her new back scratcher was even odder. A foot long, made from a weird piece of teak or other endangered wood, and at the end where the baby hand would be was a bend shaped like an L, with long fingers carved half-heartedly into the bottom. Misused, it could put out an eye.

"They let you take this through security?" I asked her.

"Why wouldn't they?" she answered. She slid the back scratcher from my hand, crossed to the dresser, and put it with the neatly folded shirts in her dresser drawer. Mother always uses the dresser drawers, no matter how short her visit, and even in a hotel. When she met me in Boston, she stayed in the hotel one night, and still she unpacked her neatly folded clothes and placed them carefully in the dresser. I didn't ask her why, because I knew she would answer:

"What's the difference to you?"

The other thing of note about Mother Mary is her suitcase. She always travels with a red canvas duffel, which she got free as part of a promotion for Marlboro cigarettes.

She used it for almost ten years, until one of the pleather handles fell off and the Marlboro red took on a carcinogenic hue.

I hate the Marlboro duffel, and on her last trip, I finally persuaded her to let me replace it. This is a nice way of saying that we fought about it all the way to the airport, so that I had exhausted her by the time we reached the Brookstone in Terminal B, where I saw my opening and didn't hesitate. I bought her a new black bag with wheels, then sat down on the floor of the store and transferred all of her clothes, including the back scratcher, into the new bag. Still she wouldn't let me throw the Marlboro bag away, but insisted that we pack it inside the Brookstone bag.

Maybe she became addicted to the Marlboro bag.

It got me thinking about suitcases, in general. I remember perfectly our family suitcase, which we used growing up. I'm going out on a limb here, but I'd bet money that you can remember the suitcase your family had when you were little.

Our family suitcase was a rigid rectangle covered with royal blue vinyl, and it had white plastic piping. Inside it were all manner of fake silk pouches with generous elastic gathering. It was so heavy only my father could carry it. And we all four used it, so either we didn't have much stuff or it was the size of Vermont.

The suitcase fascinated me, and I always imagined that someday it would be plastered with stickers in the shape of pennants, each with the name of an exotic city. Paris. Rome. Istanbul.

We went only to Atlantic City, but still.

Now nobody will grow up fascinated with their family suitcase, because everybody will remember the exact same one. A soft black box on wheels, like the one I bought at Brookstone. No decals. No tangy whiff of faraway places.

And barely enough room for a back scratcher.

Since my mother left, my back itches all the time. I got in the habit of using hers while it was here, and since she took it away, I've substituted a carving fork, a wooden spoon, and a bread knife. I ended up with a hole in my shirt and an itchy back.

Now I need to go out a buy a new back scratcher.

Preferably one with a mommy attached.

EMERGENCY HAIR

I don't know if you're like this, but here's something weird that I do.

Let's say I'm going along, not paying attention to something. Like my hair, for example. Then all of a sudden, I realize I need a haircut. Suddenly I feel as if have to get a haircut that very day, though I have ignored it for two years. I can't explain it, but a sense of urgency sweeps over me, and it means either that I need a haircut or I must escape a burning airplane, hurtling earthward.

There's no distinction in my tiny little brain.

So I call around frantically to get a hair appointment somewhere, which is always a bad idea, because it's guaranteed that I'll notice I need an emergency haircut on a Monday, when salons are closed. Don't get me started on this Monday-closing tradition, which is so entrenched that it will never change. We'll get universal health care before we get salons open on Monday, and that's backwards. Ask any woman if she'd rather have a haircut or a mammogram, and you'll see what I mean.

Anyway, if I can't get a hair appointment, I usually stop short of taking a scissors to my own hair. I'm already single enough.

Well, to stay on point, I just did the same weird thing with my house.

I have lived here for ten years, but last month, I started looking at the white stucco on my house. It needed repainting, but I hadn't repainted because I never liked the stucco in the first place. I always knew that it hid lovely tan and brown stones, because I have them on an inside wall. So last month when I saw the stucco, wheels started turning in my head. I thought, if that stucco were gone, my house could look like something out of Wyeth.

I mean Andrew, not the drug company.

Then all of a sudden, I knew the stucco had to come off. That day. If the cost were even close to reasonable, that stucco was history. If not, I'd dig it out myself with a shrimp fork.

So I went inside and started calling around like a crazy person. I managed to raise a stonemason, who came over, gave me an estimate that didn't require a second mortgage, and told me he would take the stucco off.

"Can you do it right now?" I asked.

"Are you serious?" he answered, because he didn't know me yet. About my emergency hair and all, and how I get.

So I explained, and the stonemason started the next day, which was a compromise for me. I wrote him a fat check, but it turned out to be the best money I've ever spent, if you don't count my second divorce.

The masons started jackhammering, and beautiful stonework started to show, authentic and old, which is just the look I love, as I am authentic and old myself. Every day brought new progress. The stones were tan, brown, and gold; of all shapes and sizes. I took daily cell phone photos and sent them to my friends, who stopped opening them after day three.

But then I noticed something. Next to the lovely stonework was aluminum siding. And I was pretty sure that Wyeth never painted aluminum sliding.

Let me explain.

When I bought my house, I did notice that its clapboard was unusually nice and white, but I didn't realize it was aluminum siding. I never knew that aluminum siding could look exactly like clapboard, even embossed with fake–wood grain. I didn't learn I had aluminum siding until the home inspection, but by then I was already in love with my house.

I overlook everything when I'm in love. A red flag could hit me in the nose, and I'd see only clear blue sky.

Anyway, I pried up a panel of the aluminum siding to see what was underneath. Real wooden clapboard, in need of paint, but crying for sunlight. So you know what happened next. The aluminum siding had to come off. My stonemason said he knew a contractor who could do the job and he'd get me the number.

"Right now?" I asked, but by then he knew me.

So now I have three new workmen at the house, stripping aluminum siding. The clapboard underneath is moldy and grimy, and of course, there are rotten soffits and crumbling fascia, which need to be replaced. I didn't know what a soffit or a fascia was until yesterday. Now I must have new soffits and fascia. Immediately.

And you know what's coming next.

Painters.

I can't wait.

TEMPTATION

These are hard times for people like me, who are easily tempted. I try to stay on my diet, but with all the food commercials, I find myself in a TV smorgasbord of chocolate cakes, Quarter Pounders, and vanilla ice cream. And the only way I can avoid temptation is not to buy forbidden food because if a chocolate cake finds its way into my house, I cannot resist it. I will eat my way through it. Which brings me to the point:

Illicit sex.

You may be wondering about the connection, and here it is. I was listening to the radio the other day and heard an ad for a certain website. The company slogan was, "When monogamy becomes monotony," and the pitch, delivered in a seductive female voice, was that if you're married and bored out of your mind, you're definitely entitled to an affair. Just log on.

I thought it must be a joke, or maybe I was hearing things, which was undoubtedly true, as Brad Pitt often whispers my name, in my mind.

But the next night I was watching TV and a commercial for a similar website came on. It featured a pretty girl in a negligee that women haven't worn since the days of Mamie Van Doren. The gist of her pitch was, "Married men, log on. Cheat your cheating heart out. We're cheating, too, so we won't tell."

Whoa.

I thought, this is chocolate cake of the highest order. A website for cheaters. Can human beings resist such temptation? This is like a pint of Häagen-Dasz vanilla jumping into your shopping cart, mugging you to be bought, and then spooning itself down your gullet.

This is waterboarding, with saturated fats.

In the good old days, to have an affair, you had to meet another married person at work, then court them, but that wasted a lot of precious negligee time.

Those days are over. Technology has made life easier for married people with a roving eye and a fired-up laptop.

Whoopee?

I went instantly to my computer and

logged onto the web-site, to report to you. As we all know by now, I have nobody to cheat on except a corgi. And I would never date a married man, especially one who's attracted to a screen name like easy-sexygurl.

I'm more like annoyinginterruptingurl.

On the website, the company reported that it was established in 2001 and had 1.8 million members, 8986 of whom were "on-line now!" I made a mental note that 2001 was the year the world went to hell in a handbasket and that almost 9000 people want even their cheating to be time-efficient. I bet their BlackBerrys are always on, too, and they keep them in their pants.

Their BlackBerrys, that is.

So I signed on to the service, as an Attached Female Seeking Attached Males, using an old email and fake info. I made myself age 22 and "slim" because I thought it would work better than age 52 and "can't resist chocolate cake."

Then the website gave me a choice of "Limits." Surprisingly, None was not an option. Neither was: Can't Keep My Word. Or: Thinks Integrity Makes Sense, In Theory. And not even: In Sickness And In Health, But Let's Not Get Fanatical.

Instead, the categories offered were:

Something Short Term, Something Long Term, Cyber Affairs/Erotic Chat, Whatever Excites Me, Anything Goes, and Undecided.

I chose Anything Goes. Yee-hah! In truth, I was Undecided, but that sounded like a primary voter and wouldn't project Mamie Van Doren to an Attached Male.

The next page looked like the math section of the SATs, with bar graphs showing the peak usage of the website. As you can guess, the bars showed the heaviest usage Monday through Friday, from 9 to 5. So all of this cheating was going on at the office, which made sense. Why meet in the stockroom when you can meet in the chat room? Especially if you're an Anything Goes kind of gal. At least the website would decrease cheating within the same company and distribute it among all companies, thus equalizing the market share of cheaters. Nobody wants a single business getting a cheating monopoly.

I bet Microsoft would be all over that. They hog everything.

The final page gave lots of good tips, like "Don't exaggerate your sexual abilities."

Impossible.

There was even a warning: "We have a strict policy against escorts plying their craft." Funny, I never thought of an escort as having a craft. Stonemasons have a craft. Escorts have diseases.

I clicked on the last page, which offered a book about erotic fantasies by author Sharon Sharalike. I wondered if that was her real name.

I read a little while longer, then checked my email to my fake profile. In only five minutes, I had already gotten two emails, both from Attached Males, age 47 and 51, respectively. By the way, remember I'm 22. In my dreams. And theirs.

The first Attached Male liked candles, and the second had an "insatiable sex drive." Both described themselves as "fit." And both wanted Something Long Term.

Something Long Term?

Isn't that marriage?

I wonder what their wives wanted.

KIDS SAY THE DARNDEST

I'm a fan of shortcuts. Not in my job, but in everything else, to make more time for my job. Daughter Francesca calls me Sally Shortcut, but it only makes me swell with pride. I don't know who raised that child.

Most of the time, I get away with taking a shortcut. This morning, however, my shortcut required the calling of squad cars, the stopping of traffic on a major road, and me running for five miles with a bucket of carrots.

Let me explain.

Remember Buddy, My Little Pony? He's a brown-and-white paint, and I ride him for fun. Actually, I walk him for fun. He's twenty-five years old and he goes no faster than a herky-jerky stutter-step. He's the Walter Brennan of ponies.

In fact, I doubted that Buddy still had a gallop in him, until this morning. When he morphed into Secretariat.

I ride with a group of other women, which means we sit on our butts and yap while the horses do all the work. Buddy is the oldest, smallest, and fattest of all the horses, usually the Steady Eddie on our trail rides, which go around cornfields and through woods, ending when we're tired of yammering.

I mean, exercising.

You may recall that I take shortcuts clipping Buddy, which he accepts with the grudging resignation of Eeyore. I had clipped him before the winter, and when the first nice day of spring arrived, I decided to go for a ride. I slipped off his blanket, but to my dismay, Buddy had returned to his mastodon self. I had no time to clip him, and I thought, I can take a shortcut.

I headed out for a ride with friend Paula, who has a gentle giant Percheron named Dave. Dave and Buddy are paints with the same coloring, like Mutt and Jeff, only horses. By the way, I hope you're following my references. Young or sane people may have to use Google.

So Paula and I were on horseback, walking along in the sunshine, chatting away, when I noticed that Buddy was shaking his head more than usual. As furry as he was, he looked like one of those automatic shoeshine brushes they have in hotels.

"I guess he's a little itchy," I said. "I didn't have time to clip him."

"He looks cute, all furry," Paula said, which is only one of the many things I like about her. But in the next minute, her eyes widened and she shouted, "Watch out, he's gonna roll!"

And before I knew what was happening, Buddy was sinking onto his knees and rolling onto the grass to scratch his back. The only problem was, I was still in the saddle.

Now I'm no horsewoman, as you're about to find out, because I didn't even realize what was happening until Paula told me and I remembered some faint instruction that you should never stay on the back of a rolling horse, unless you like the sensation of 1500 pounds landing on your pelvis, knee, and ankle. In other words, I jumped off like a crazy person and let out a scream. It freaked Buddy out, and he looked back, showing the whites of his eyes and so terrified that he leapt up and galloped away. He tore across the cornfield, and in no time, became a fuzzy black dot, like a period with hair.

I couldn't believe it. I blinked and blinked. Paula and Dave blinked and blinked. And then I had to do something because Buddy was galloping toward the busiest street in the neighborhood. Either he would dent a truck or a truck would dent him. So I started screaming and running and calling 911 all at once.

"Your emergency please?" the dispatcher asked, and I kept running through the cornfield, screaming for Buddy and telling the story, like this:

"I always take shortcuts but maybe it isn't such a good idea all the time!"

"Pardon?"

Amazingly enough, five minutes later there were three police cars blocking traffic, five armed cops, Paula, Dave, and six volunteers from a nearby horse farm, who brought a plastic bucket of carrots, intended to entice runaway ponies. We chased Buddy everywhere, and he ignored us, tearing all over the cornfield in curlicues and loop-the-loops, until I was pretty sure that he was spelling something or making crop circles.

We chased him until we were exhausted and he finally trapped himself behind a fence, just short of the road and certain death.

And so it ended happily, thanks to Paula, Dave, Good Samaritans, and the local constabulary.

Except for one thing: daughter Francesca was right.

Again.

THE FIXER

You may remember that I'm in Home Improvement Frenzy. Aluminum siding is coming off, cedar shakes are going on. Working at my house today are stonemasons, roofers, and carpenters, but none of them is single.

It gets worse.

Yesterday morning after it rained hard, a stonemason hurried in to tell me that my levee was broken. He was upset. So was I. I didn't know I had a levee. I didn't even know what a levee was. All I knew about levees was that somebody drove his Chevy to the levee but the levee was dry.

"How bad is a broken levee?" I asked.

"Very bad." He told me that when my levee broke, my springhouse got flooded, and because I have a well, that probably meant I had no running water.

"Really?" I crossed to the faucet and turned it on, but only a tiny stream of water came out. "Uh oh."

"You need an excavator."

You can imagine how this news delighted me. I was already fixing everything that could be fixed on the house, and I had been so worried that I would be limited in the amount of money I could spend on home repair. I didn't realize that I could spend money fixing the ground, too.

Yay!

My ground was broken, and suddenly the possibilities were limitless. I could spend and spend and spend, especially if the next thing to break was the sky. I could hire carpenters to build a wooden frame and support heaven itself. And after I had repaired the earth and the sky, I could move on to the sea.

I hear the tides need holding back.

So, to come back to the point, I learned that a levee is a mound of dirt that holds water in a channel, to control the runoff. If you live in the suburbs, you know about runoff. Runoff belongs with words like *aggravated assault* and *tax increase.* Runoff can make even sane citizens take up clubs, and if you start a conversation with a suburban type on the subject, be ready to settle in for the duration. Ranting will be involved, fists shaken, and development decried. Also revenuers, then gov'mint in general.

I had to get my runoff under control, and fast. One of my contractors knew a guy who knew an excavator, so the excavator came and gave me an estimate to repair the levee. It would cost $10,000.

Ouchie.

I gazed at my broken levee, wondering if I could get a shovel and do it myself. As far as I could tell, a side of a hill had washed away and the dirt had to be dug out and piled back up again. It wasn't rocket science. I could make a gutter, like in a bowling alley. Or like the moat around a sandcastle, at the beach. I mean, how hard could it be?

But assistant Laura reminded me that I have a job and told me to get another estimate.

"Do I have to?" I asked her.

"Of course."

Now here's another thing. I don't usually get a lot of estimates. I don't have time, and basically, I trust people. I know that labor costs money and so do materials. Everybody's entitled to make a living, and I have found that people are fair and honest.

"Get real," Laura said, so I listened to her, as I do in all things. I called a second excavator, who came over and gave me a second estimate. His cost?

$1000.

To review: two excavators, one estimate at $10,000 and one at $1000. For the same job.

You can imagine how delighted I was to hear this news, which showed me another way to spend even more and more and more money. As much as I was spending to fix my house, I could be spending ten times as much with no extra effort. All I had to do was hire the right contractors.

I called Laura and told her. "Can you believe it?"

"Yes."

"Now what do I do?"

"Get another estimate. You need three."

"Yes, master."

I hung, up, excited. Maybe I could get an estimate for $100,000. I wanted a top quality levee. A prestige levee. One that you'd need a Mercedes to drive to. And it would never, ever run dry.

So I went online looking for a third excavator, letting my imagination run free. Outside my window, I noticed that the clouds were looking a little gray. Dingy. They needed a fresh coat of white paint. The cost would be in the prep. Power-washing, burning, caulking, priming. It would cost a fortune to paint the clouds.

I'm on it, people.

MONA LUCY SMILE

I just lived an episode of *Emergency Vet.* Tune in.

The star is Lucy, my old golden retriever, who is still rockin' after thirteen years. Her eyes, brown as bitter-sweet chocolate, remain bright, though her step has slowed and she scuffs around on dust-mop paws. Her fur, which used to be a thick russet color, never grew back after a shave last summer, so her coat sprouts in crazy patches, like onion grass.

Lucy's a Bad Hair Dog.

Our story opens when I notice that Lucy has a wound on her chest. It's hidden by matted chest hair, and it's yucky, a medical term you may know.

So I take her to our vet who biopsies the yuckiness and it turns out to be skin cancer, though an X-ray shows that it hasn't spread. This qualifies as good news, except that during the week after the yuckiness, Lucy ages in fast-forward. She walks so slowly she's almost in reverse and sleeps so deeply I hold my breath until I see hers. By Wednesday, I worry that this is The End. By Friday, Lucy cannot stand up without help, and I take her to the vet.

I'm sure this is The End.

But my vet is the greatest in the world, and he thinks it may be a spinal degenerative condition. He puts her on steroids and tells me to worry only if there's a downturn. He thinks it's not The End, and I love him for that. I believe him until the next morning, when Lucy's front legs fail, too.

Your basic downturn.

She breathes more heavily, blinks all the time, and seems disoriented. I have seen dying before, and it looks just like this.

Complicating the plot is that daughter Francesca is in California on spring break, and she is devoted to this dog. If this is The End, she has a right to know. So I call her, and she gets on a series of planes, spending almost fifteen hours in the air to get home in time to say good-bye. When I meet her at the airport on Monday afternoon, estrogen flows freely.

On Monday evening, we take the dog back to the vet, who examines her while I give the headline. Francesca fills in the details, about how the dog's face is so different, which is new since our last visit. I hadn't noticed it at all; I was too focused on Lucy's other problems. That she wasn't so cute anymore didn't matter.

"Interesting," the vet says, poking around, and as Francesca goes on, I'm hearing a child talk about her dearest pet. She loves everything about this dog, and if there is such a thing as a novelist's keen eye for detail, she has it. I don't. To me, Lucy is a red dog who needs Rogaine.

Francesca is saying to the vet, "She's a beautiful dog. She doesn't look like this. Something's wrong with her face."

"Like what?" asks the vet, whom I sense is humoring her. I marvel at how kind people are, when it counts.

Francesca continues, "Her smile doesn't pull back that way. See how her lips are tense? Like they're frozen?"

The vet looks up. "Please excuse me a minute." Then she leaves the room and returns five minutes later with a book that she sets down on the examining table. She points to a picture on the open page, and it shows a black dog, smiling exactly like Lucy.

"That's what she looks like!" Francesca says, and the vet nods.

"It's called *risus sardonicus,* which is Latin

for sardonic smile. Your dog has lockjaw. Tetanus. That's why her back legs are failing. The smile tipped me off."

I look over, amazed. "Dogs get tetanus? How?" I'm thinking of rusty nails.

"They do but it's incredibly rare. I've never seen a case. They get it from an open wound."

I'm remembering the yuckiness, prior. "So now what happens?"

"You need to see a specialist."

So the next morning we're at a specialist, who qualifies as the nicest doggie neurologist in the country, because he takes one look at our wacky hairless dog and says, "Hello, gorgeous."

You know what I checked. Of course, he's married.

He confirms that Lucy has tetanus, which is so rare that he wants to take a video of it. He tells us that antibiotics will cure her. That not only is she going to live, her paralysis will arrest and she'll be able to walk again in a month.

We are smiling. So is Lucy, albeit sardonically.

Francesca is going back to school.

I am going back to work.

Not The End.

Color Me Mine

I'm two months from getting the house painted, but I'm already fantasizing about paint colors. If the real estate classifieds are porn, paint chips are a kinky subculture, the S & M of home décor.

The pain is exquisite.

My fantasies began when my painter dropped off a big black case that contained huge books of paint chips. I'm not dumb, I've seen the paint chips that you get from Home Depot, but I've never seen one of these books. Each one weighs about three pounds, and the paint chips are bolted together with a single fastener, so you can slide the chips out to make a circle, like a merry-go-round of color. The painter gave me three books, each with hundreds of pages, and each page has seven paint chips. By my calculation, this equals four billion eleventy-seven gillion different colors.

It hurts so good.

In no time, I'm sliding the paint chips out in a circle, the tangerines overlapping the marigolds, the cobalts eclipsing the limes, the pinks complementing the purples, all the colors fanning out from the center, making a 360° fountain of acrylic excitement.

I had no idea what color I wanted to paint the house, but all of a sudden, the books opened up a spectrograph of chromatic possibilities. The paint chips whirled together like spin art on the boardwalk, and all the colors of the rainbow were mine. I flashed on a childhood filled with Crayola crayons, from the starter eight to the big-girl double-layers of sixty-four. I thought of old-fashioned tins of watercolor paints, with rectangular wells for dirty water. I could paint the house any color I wanted, and the thought made me giddy.

There was nobody around to exercise good judgment. No saner head to prevail.

Yippee!

I should point out that there is precedent for my temporary color insanity. After my second divorce, I painted my kitchen the color of vitamin C, merely because nobody could stop me.

So I gazed at the paint chips and imagined golden shutters against the tan fieldstone of the house. Creamy ivory clapboard in the sunshine. Colonial molding painted classy forest green. Fascia the gentle hue of daffodils. I spent hours looking at the colors in all different kinds of light and made lists of the letters and numbers on each paint chip, a cryptic code that added to its tantalizing mystery. For example, Corinthian White was OC-111. I looked in vain for the meaning of OC, but the book kept its secrets.

I even found myself carried away by the names of the colors, some of which were delicious. I imagined shutters of Sharp Cheddar (2017-20). I considered doing the trim in Pale Celery (OC-114) and Carrot Stick (2016-30), low-carb colors. I could finish my molding in Peach Sorbet (2015-40), which was like eating windowsills for dessert.

Some color names struck an emotional chord, as in True Blue (2066-50), and others were adorable, like Tricycle Red (2000-20). Growing up, I had a red tricycle and a red wagon. I looked for a color named Red Wagon, but there was none. I made a mental note to email Benjamin Moore.

Still other names made me think of vacations — Caribbean Coast (2065-60), South Beach (2043-50), and Blue Wave (2065-50). But Asbury Sand (2156-40) didn't look any different from Serengeti Sand (2164-40), and it's probably easier to get a hotel in Jersey.

I was bothered by the names that made no sense. What's a Jeweled Peach (2013-30)? Or Smoke Embers (AC-28)? There's no such thing as smoke embers. Smoke comes from embers. Anyway, it was a Boring Gray. And between us, Adobe Dust (2175-40) looks suspiciously like the dirt under my bed, which I call Philadelphia Filth.

Still other color names were a little precious. Roasted Sesame Seed (2160-40) isn't a color, it's a recipe. Mantis Green (2033-60) is just plain creepy. Dollar Bill Green (2050-30) is for pimps only.

Some color names confused me. Nantucket Gray (HC-111) is green. Gypsy Love (2085-30) is maroon, which has nothing to do with either Gypsies or Love. Soft Cranberry (2094-40), which should be maroon, is beige. And Milkyway (OC-110) is white like milk, not brown like the candy or black like the galaxy.

Kelp Forest Green (2043-30) is distinctly unhelpful. Shore House Green (2047-50) begs the question. Cherokee Brick (2082-30) is historically inaccurate. Distant Gray (2124-70) is emotionally unavailable. Amber Waves (2159-40) panders in an election year. There was no Purple Mountains Majesty.

Other names reveal that whoever thought them up was drunk. There is no other explanation for Perky Peach (2012-50), Springy Peach (2011-60), or Limesickle (2145-50). Maybe they were drinking Moonshine (2140-60).

By the end, I was supersaturated with color, hues, and tints, dizzy from my myriad paint fantasies. But at least I found the perfect color for the house.

White.

THE ACCIDENTAL DRIVER

Insurance is fun. I don't mean health insurance, because health insurance is never fun. But for some reason, car insurance is a laugh riot.

Here's what I mean.

Amazingly enough, I have never been in an accident, if you don't count my two marriages.

For all this time, I've been paying lots of dough in car insurance, in the hope that someday I'll get creamed and it will pay off. But so far, no good.

I made my first claim ten years ago, when this happened: I used to have a gate at the end of my driveway, and when I left, I'd get out of the car, open the gate, and drive through, then close it behind me. One day, I stopped the car, got out, and opened the gate, but before I could get back in, a gust of wind came from nowhere and blew the gate into my car, denting it while I stood by and used profanity.

I put in a claim, to finally get my money's worth from my car insurance, but they said that I wasn't covered for hitting my gate.

I disagreed. "I didn't hit my gate. My gate hit me."

Silence, from the other end of the phone.

"I have a point, you know."

And I won, which means that, after my deductible, they paid me $38, and I had only $1,328,373,730.92 left to get my money's worth. Perhaps if you have a swinging gate, I could park nearby.

That's why I was delighted last month when I was driving on the highway and suddenly heard a loud *pock,* and five miles later, noticed a crack in my windshield. Five miles after that, the crack extended several jagged inches, and five after that, it looked like a sales chart in a bad year.

Yay!

I was so happy I could make another claim. Mind you, my second in thirty years. So I called the insurance company. "Remember me? This time, a rock hit me, and I need a new windshield. Am I covered?"

"Yes, of course." She proceeded to tell me that I could get a new windshield from one of three places, which sounded like Clem's Windshields, Windshields R' Us, and Just

Windshields.

I didn't like that. "But I want the same windshield. Can't I just take it back to the dealer?"

"No, you have to use our approved vendors."

"What is this, an HMO for cars? If so, I want Personal Choice."

"Okay, but that'll cost you more."

"Isn't $1,328,373,730.92 enough?"

Silence, from the other end of the phone.

Life insurance is even more fun. I pay lots of dough every month, but I never seem to die. Then last month, the agent called to tell me that my life insurance policy was about to "convert." I had no idea what she was talking about, but the bottom line was that the insurance I've had all this time is about to end, because now I'm old enough to need it.

Thanks.

I gather my demise wasn't in the original deal, which was that I would pay lots of dough every month for no earthly reason, even though I was healthy as a horse and in no danger of harm from anything except gates and rocks.

They call that term insurance, but I think they should call it joke insurance. They sold it to me because they knew I wouldn't need it. They were only joking.

So now I have to buy new life insurance, which will cost me triple what the old insurance cost, because I have sprung various and sundry leaks. They call this whole life insurance because it will cost me my whole life. Unless I die tomorrow, in which case the joke is on them.

Cross your fingers.

Honestly, it's worth it to me. Strike me dead. Bring it, now. I want my epitaph to read, SHOW ME THE MONEY.

So I began investigating new life insurance policies, which is when the agent told me that I needed disability insurance, too. When I asked why, she answered, "Because you make your living using your brain."

"Thank you," I replied. Evidently, she doesn't read me. "So what's your point?"

"If you incurred brain damage, you couldn't work, and that's why you need disability insurance."

I disagreed. I didn't think anything could damage my brain more than thinking about insurance does. "I could work if I hurt my arm."

"True."

"I could work if I hurt my leg."

"Also true," she said. "But what if you were in a car accident?"

"I've never had a car accident. Gates and rocks are gunning for me, but that's not the same thing."

"Then you're very lucky."

I disagreed. "I bought car insurance and life insurance and now you want me to buy disability insurance. I paid thousands of dollars for decades, for no conceivable reason. You call that lucky? Should I buy flood insurance, even though I live on a hill? Or planet insurance, for when Mars attacks? Or third marriage insurance, in case I lose my mind again?"

Silence, from the other end of the phone.

MIX 'N MATCH

These are confusing times to be alive, biologically speaking. All manner of shenanigans are going on at DNA level, so many I can't keep up with all them all. I rely on People magazine to keep me abreast of the latest science news, and I was amazed by its article on the pregnant man.

You may have heard about him, a transgendered male who is six months pregnant. I couldn't figure out from the story which equipment he was born with, and by the middle of the story, I didn't care. The headline read, HE'S HAVING A BABY, and that was enough for me. A man can get pregnant?

This is one great idea, if you ask me.

I mean, why not?

My pregnancy involved a fifty-pound weight gain, water retention, chubby ankles, and a weird rash on my belly that itched like crazy. Pregnant, I was no Demi Moore on the cover of *Vanity Fair.* I wasn't even Christina Aguilera on the cover of *Marie Claire.* Or Britney Spears on the cover of *Bazaar.* Pregnant, I should have been on the cover of *This Old House.*

If men want to get pregnant, I say, be my guest. So what if the photos look funny, with a mustache and a pregnant belly? It wouldn't be the first time. I come from a proud line of mustachioed women.

Don't split hairs.

In fact, I'm encouraging all you men out there to get pregnant, right away. Give your marriage a boost. Do your wife a favor. You've probably got a pretty long Honey-Do list sitting on the kitchen counter, waiting for you. I bet that, in most house holds, HAVE BABY FOR ME would shoot right up to *numero uno.* You wouldn't have to take out the trash or mow the lawn for the rest of your life.

And think of the guilt you could inflict! Men getting pregnant makes much more sense, especially when it comes to delivery. Men are man enough to give birth, by definition. In fact, men probably wouldn't bat an eye. I bet if you put them in front of a TV during playoff season, they wouldn't even notice they were in labor. Women could get them ice chips for their beer and run downfield with the receiving blanket, and men could pop the babies out like footballs.

Score!

And pregnant men aren't the only biological advance, of late. Another is cows that give skim milk. I read online that scientists in the UK were able to do this recently, and isn't that another great idea? Nobody needs an obsolete cow that produces fattening milk. That's like buying Cow 1.0 when Cow 4.0 is already on the market.

Plus, it turns out that butter from the latest and greatest cows has the advantage of being spreadable straight from the refrigerator.

Now we're talking. I hate it when you have to wait for the butter to soften. We all do. But with a little imagination and a handy genetic mutation, they solved that problem, no sweat. I hope those scientists in the UK get back on the stick and whip us up a cow that produces Diet Coke. After all, how many grown-ups are drinking milk by the glass? I down a couple of Diet Cokes a day, and a cow that could squirt soda would suit me much better, as long as it was decaf.

Or why not think outside of the box? How about a cow that produces gin and tonic? I could drink from one of those cows all day.

But we couldn't let the pregnant men near one.

Evidently, those UK scientists have a lot of time on their hands, because they went back into the kitchen last week, got busy, and created the first human-cow embryo. I'm not kidding. I read it online. It might even be on Wikipedia by now. If it isn't, you can put it there, citing this as authority.

I have a question about the human-cow embryo. Why did they pick that combination? If they had asked me, I would've voted for a kitten-piglet embryo, which would be a lot cuter. Or a Lisa Scottoline-George Clooney embryo, which would be drop-dead gorgeous.

Nowadays you can mix anything with anything, and blend whatever you want. It's like Cold Stone Creamery, with eggs and sperms.

So let's get crazy. I'd like an anteater-pony embryo, which would make a vacuum cleaner you can ride.

Or a dog-cat embryo, which would make a cat that adores you. Or a dog that hates your guts.

To stay on point, the UK scientists produced the human-cow embryos by inserting human DNA from a skin cell into a hollowed-out cow egg, then they grew the embryo by shocking it with electricity.

I saw that once in a Frankenstein movie. Maybe that's where they got the idea.

But did they forget the ending?

THINGS TO DO

I just finished my next book, which means that I finally have time to tackle my list of Things To Do. It takes me a year to write a book, so I had 293,773 Things to Do. I started doing them on Saturday, but I got only one Thing done.

It's not my fault.

To explain, I let my Things To Do pile up because when I'm in the final draft of a book, I do nothing else. I let everything go, including my roots. You don't want to see me with final-draft roots. It looks like my hair got caught in a forest fire, leaving behind burnt trunks and a very single woman.

We begin our story when my driver's license expired. It expired last July, because, like I told you, I let everything go. I didn't even know it had expired until last month, when I tried to fly out of town for a library gig and the security lady at the airport

229

noticed it. I talked fast and got the real-deal search, and they let me fly. Then I had another flight the week after, for another library gig, so to avoid the expired license problem, I grabbed my passport.

But my passport had expired.

Like I told you, I let everything go.

So I'm at the airport and I'm showing the security lady my expired license and expired passport, and after much fast-talking by me, head-shaking by her, and a no-joke background check, they let me fly.

So you get it. When I finished my book, I sent away to renew my driver's license, but I needed to get my photo taken to renew my passport, which brings me to my first Thing To Do, on Saturday morning.

I went to get my picture taken at my local post office, but was surprised to find that it closed at 11:30 A.M. I knew there was another post office nearby, so I drove over and arrived at noon. To my surprise, it had just closed, too. A woman walking by told me that another post office was open later, so I headed over, but traffic was busy with people doing their Things To Do, and I didn't get there until 1:00 P.M., and you guessed it.

They were closing.

Surprise!

I ran inside before they could lock me out, and they said that I should come back on Monday — but only from 9:30 A.M. to 11:30 A.M., which is when they take the passport photos.

I didn't ask when they lick the stamps or weigh the mail. I suspect that happens between 10:12 A.M. and 12:01 P.M., depending on your zip code, weight, and zodiac sign.

By the way, the other two post offices nearby closed at 3:00 P.M. and 4:00 P.M., respectively. So, to review, we're talking about five post offices with five different closing times.

Huh? And more importantly, wha?

Don't get me started on why the post office closes at all on Saturday, which is the only day that the gainfully employed can go. And never mind that they assign store hours in a way that guarantees you'll have zero chance of remembering which end is up. We won't get into it because, in fairness, it's not only the post office that thwarts our Things To Do.

It's everybody, conspiring against us. We have more and more Things To Do, and all the stores are finding new and creative ways not to help us Do our Things. In fact, the worst culprits are the stores that make us

Do *their* Things.

Observe.

It started harmlessly enough, back in the eighties. If you went to a salad bar, you had to make your own salad. And at the gas station, you had to pump your own gas.

Then it went crazy.

Nowadays, at the food store, you not only bag your own groceries and take them to the car, but you also check yourself out. You can even bring your own bags.

They still supply the food, so they can call it a food store, and not a Bring-Your-Own-Food Store & Do-Our-Jobs-For-Us Emporium.

You can go to a car wash, where you can wash your car yourself. Or the hairdresser, where you can dry your own hair. Or the train station, where you can buy your ticket yourself. Or the airport, where you can get your own boarding pass.

They still fly the plane.

For now.

To send a package, you can print out your own air bills. And at the fast food restaurants, they give you a paper cup and tell you to get your own soda.

You have my point?

There is no way we have a chance of getting done with all our Things To Do. Not if we can only do one Thing on a Saturday, and that's between 9:23 A.M. and 10:18 A.M., if the moon is in the seventh house and Jupiter's aligned with Mars.

And you're a Libra.

We have way too many Things To Do, especially if you add their Things to our Things.

It's easier to write a book.

LUCY

Sad news, and this time it's no joke.

My old dog Lucy, who was happily recovering from tetanus, just passed away. This time her heart failed, and she died the day my story about her amazing recovery appeared in the newspaper. I got home from the vet hospital, without her, in time to pick up the Sunday paper.

I didn't read it.

I won't go on at length about Lucy, except to say that she was a wonderful dog. You may remember John Grogan's great book about Marley, the "bad" dog he loved so much. Well, Lucy wasn't Marley. She was a saint, in the form of a golden retriever.

She did all the things dogs are supposed to do. She was always loving and happy. She learned her words. She sat and stayed with pride. She followed her people everywhere. She snored with gusto. I never minded her snoring, although Thing Two always hated it. I swear, the night he threw her out of the bedroom for snoring was the beginning of the end for me. Six months later, he was gone, and she was back in place.

She grew up with daughter Francesca and was devoted to her. Lucy let herself be ridden around the house like a pony, dressed in T-shirts and makeshift bonnets, and had a piece of paper stuffed in her collar, making a cape for a Superdog. She even had her toenails painted pink.

Lucy looked damn good in pink.

She slept upstairs and never came down until Francesca did, even if my daughter slept until late, as teenagers are wont do.

And Lucy had many talents. She could reach anything on any counter, no matter how far back you put it. If you forgot you left food on the table, she never did. She could locate a carbohydrate with the accuracy of a doggie GPS system. She never destroyed or damaged anything. She never had an accident on the rug. She could rough-house with the other dogs, yet be mild when a baby was around. She was friendly to UPS and FedEx people, but she was never pushy to get affection. She'd come up beside you and lean against you, warming the outside of your knee.

Though she was good, Lucy was no

goody-goody. Once she bolted from obedience class after Francesca, who had left to go to the bathroom.

She didn't care much for rules. She made her own. Which is the only nub of resentment I have this morning, at the way she died. I had been away for the weekend visiting Francesca, and when I left Lucy and the gang with a dog sitter, she was doing fine. I came home last night to find her breathing labored. She wagged her tail when she saw me, but didn't get up. And she hadn't eaten in a day.

So I got her in the car and drove her to my great vet, who made time to see her, even at closing. The vet heard a heart arrhythmia and thought she needed emergency bloodwork and tests done, so I left there and drove to the emergency vet's, which is nearby. Lucy breathed hard in the back seat, her head flopped listlessly between her paws, her neck stretched out more than usual. I knew she was dying, even in the car. I could see it. This time, there would be no surprise diagnosis or magic pill.

When we got to the hospital, amazingly, she rallied and walked out of the car, wagging her tail at the nurse.

To Lucy, a stranger was just a very new friend.

So I explained to the nurse that I thought she was dying, and the nurse took the leash and told me she'd come back to give me a report. I said that I wanted to go in with Lucy while they examined her, but they said no.

It was against the rules.

I made a fuss. If they couldn't save Lucy, I wanted to be with her. But the nurse promised to come get me if things took a turn for the worse. For a minute, I didn't know what to do. I looked at all the upset faces of the people in the waiting room and knew I was making a scene. Lucy stood between the nurse and me, wagging her tail. Because she doesn't sweat the small stuff.

So I let her go.

She left happily through the swinging steel doors, and I sat down and stared at a magazine.

I was remembering the day my father died. I knew he was going to die, and when his heart gave out, after a battle with cancer, our hospital room flooded with at least thirty doctors, four of whom went to his bed and tried to save his life, while all the rest were there as observers, edging us out of the way, to the far wall. Brother Frank fought through them to hold my father's hand, and I hugged my stepmother as she cried, and at some point somebody told us to leave.

"No," I said. "I'm not going anywhere."

A woman doctor, who was observing, turned around and said to me, "But unnecessary people aren't supposed to be in the room."

She actually said that. I'm not making it up. I could never write such bad fiction.

You know what I said to her? I said, "He's my father, and you don't even know him. Who's unnecessary?"

And so I got to be present when my father left this earth, which is the least I owed him.

With Lucy, I wasn't in the room yet, so I let them keep me out. I tried to fight, but I didn't want to make a scene.

My heart failed.

So I sat down and waited, and not ten minutes later, a different nurse rushed out, looking for the owner of "the golden."

Because they didn't know her.

And I got to be with Lucy at the very very end, which is the least I owed her. I don't know if she knew I was there. The vets tell me yes, and they were nice people, trying to save her life and following the hospital's rules. It wasn't their fault. I don't blame them, and I even thanked them for all they did. But after being with Lucy for all of her thirteen years, I hated being excluded from her last ten minutes.

Next time, I'm kicking those doors open.

And the truth is, it hardly matters much, the next day. Maybe they didn't know Lucy, but I did. Francesca did. So did my mother and brother.

And now, you do, too.

And yes, she was golden.

JUST DANDY

I have detected another difference between men and women, in addition to the one you're thinking of.

Before I begin, the credit for this observation goes to best friend Franca. She told it to me the other day, and I agreed. That's the great thing about having a best friend. We agree on everything. In fact, I can't recall the last time we disagreed about anything, and Franca would be my first phone call after I murdered someone. She wouldn't even ask why I did it. She would know I had an excellent reason. She'd just drive over with a shovel and a Hefty bag, no question.

A best friend is just another name for accessory after the fact.

I would do it for her, too, though Franca's too nice to kill anyone. She's the good twin to my evil.

So here's what happened.

Franca lives in the suburbs and she loves this time of year, when dandelions appear on her front lawn. We agree about loving dandelions. We're not dumb, we know that they're weeds, but that's a technicality, isn't it? They're beautiful, and where do you draw the line between weeds and wildflowers? And if it's a pretty weed, grows naturally, and costs nothing, why don't we welcome it?

Don't start in with the fact that dandelions kill grass. There's room on the planet for both dandelions and grass. In fact, I think it's high time that grass learned to share.

But it turns out that some of the people in Franca's neighborhood don't like dandelions, and they're men. One of them knocked on her door to suggest that his lawn guy could give her an estimate on getting rid of her dandelions, and another left a bag of Weed N Feed at her door. She thinks they were trying to do something nice, but I'm not sure. If someone left a six-pack of Slim-Fast on my doorstep, I wouldn't see the upside.

The dandelion issue reminded me of scenes from my second marriage, which is like watching a horror movie without the Raisinets. Thing Two liked the lawn to be dandelion-free, so we paid somebody to strew pretty balls of poison all over the grass, like nightmare Skittles. They made the yard reek of high-school swimming pool and left greasy spots on the front walk. Plus I worried that the dogs would eat them and grow a fifth leg.

Sadly, the dandelions went away, and happily, so did Thing Two.

Now my dandelions grow freely, bright splotches of yellow dotting the green lawn. They make me happy every time I see them. I love them so much I might paint my shutters that color, which Benjamin Moore calls Mellow Yellow (2020-50).

Franca likes dandelions even after they've changed to balls of wispy seeds. She reminded me that when our kids were little, we used to pull the dandelions, make a wish, and blow the seeds into the wind. She said that her lawn is full of "fuzzy heads of wishes" and when she looks at it, she sees the "magic of our babies' childhoods."

I told you she was the good twin.

And really, who hasn't wished on a dandelion? Wouldn't the world be a better place if there were less Weed N Feed and more wishes?

I wonder if this difference over dandelions applies to lawns in general. Thing Two was fetishistic about the lawn, and assistant

Laura tells the story of the day her sons were playing wiffleball and her husband felt bugged that home plate was messing up the grass. Laura told him, "We're not raising grass, we're raising boys."

He agreed, and he likes dandelions, too.

So I can't decide if this is a boy/girl thing or not. I'm curious about what you think.

And I wonder what this means for buttercups.

GRADUATION DAY

Daughter Francesca is graduating from college, and I spent the last hour trying to figure out her school's incredibly complicated commencement schedule. According to the website, there are three separate commencement exercises, and the main one will be attended by "approximately 32,000 people." The gates open at 6:45 A.M., and not everyone will get a seat, so the website advises me to get there in advance.

Ya think?

And how exactly do you play musical chairs with a small city?

And how early should I get there — 1986?

Nor does the website advise how to wake up my 83-year-old mother at that hour, much less provide her with the requisite coffee and apple fritter from Dunkin' Donuts. Our fancy hotel doesn't serve breakfast until 6:00 A.M. and it offers items like steel-cut oatmeal imported from Ireland and omelets with organic eggs. The website doesn't seem to understand that if you try to sell my mother a $30 breakfast, she will throw it at you.

The website also states that the commencement exercises will be held outside, but neither does it state how to get my mother to walk on grass, which she regards as exercise and therefore against her religion. Nor can the website conceive of how slowly Mother Mary walks. The hotel is only three blocks away, but she will have to leave two days prior to make it by dawn.

The solution would be for her to skip the first graduation ceremony and attend only the second ceremony, which will be smaller, attended by only ten thousand people. But the website gives no clue as to how to find her in a crowd that size, as she is only four foot eleven inches tall and the oldest member of the Lollipop Guild.

She'd stand out if she wore her lab coat, but then she could end up at the medical school graduation.

In theory, brother Frank could escort her to the second ceremony, but that would require him to find me in a warren of colonial brick dorms, all of which look alike and are badly signed, the better to keep out the unwashed. Like the Scottolines, until

Francesca got in.

The other possibility is that my mother goes to the third graduation ceremony, to which alumni and bigwigs are invited because that's where the celebrity intellectual is speaking. The only problem is, the third ceremony has nothing to do with my daughter, and to us, she's the celebrity intellectual.

The fourth option is that my mother waits in the hotel and watches all three ceremonies on the local cable TV, but for that she could have stayed in Miami and not missed her personal marathon of *Law & Order.*

So I'm confused.

I need an advanced degree to figure out how to deal with college graduation. Or maybe a chart with color-coded highlighting or a map with flag pins. But maybe all this confusion is good, because it distracts me from the larger topic — that my daughter is graduating from college.

Of course it's an enormously happy occasion, and it goes without saying that I'm proud of her. It doesn't go without saying *to* her. I tell her how proud I am at least three times a day and I think every kid needs to hear it, even big girls in caps and gowns. But what I mean is that while I'm so happy with the fact that she's graduating, we haven't had a chance yet to talk about where she's going to live until she finds a job. You know my answer:

Home.

Or better yet, in a convent.

Now that college is over, it seems only right that she should move home and get back into her diapers.

I mean, that was the deal, right?

I let my kid go to college, now she should come home. It's only fair, even though I have enjoyed being an empty nester, and it seems like only yesterday I wrote about missing her. Well, I do, and now I want her back. When I told this to a friend of mine, she told me a joke:

What's the difference between an Italian mother and a Rottweiler?

The Rottweiler eventually lets go.

So college graduation is good news and bad news. The good news is that my kid is healthy, happy, and now, well-educated. And the bad news is that her life is beginning, without me in earnest, so that boo-hoo-my-kid-is-going-to-college was only a step in the separation that began when they cut the umbilical cord.

That was my first mistake. I should have stopped them, right there. In my view, it was medical malpractice.

And after the initial snip, the separation proceeded incrementally to first step, then first date, first car, and first degree. She's beginning her life as an adult, on her own.

I guess they call it commencement for a reason.

And so we will attend, our raggedy and irregular little family, there to bear witness at this awesome event. I can picture it now. The golden girl we all raised, beautiful in cap and billowing gown. We will bring roses too cumbersome to hold. We will shift on hard wooden chairs. Mother Mary won't be able to hear or see anything, yet she will weep. We all will. It will be an estrogen fest. Thank God that brother Frank is gay, so he can join in.

And back at the hotel, Ruby The Corgi will be ordering the imported oatmeal.

Nothing but the best, on this very, very special day.

Congratulations, Francesca.

We're proud of you.

TROUBLE IN PARADISE

Mother Mary and brother Frank were getting ready to fly up for daughter Francesca's graduation when trouble broke out in Miami. It began when I got a text from Frank, which read:

CALL ME ASAP ABOUT MOM.

I freak out. Mother Mary isn't in the best of health, and Frank never texts me. I grab the phone and speed-dial him. "What's the matter? Is she okay?"

"It's really bad." He sounds upset, and my heart pounds in my chest.

"What happened?"

"I got a tattoo."

Huh? "And she had a heart attack?"

"No, she won't speak to me. She won't even look at me. She turns her head when I go to kiss her cheek."

My blood pressure returns to normal, though I still don't understand. "This is what you texted me about? This is nothing!"

"Really? You try living with her."

An excellent point. The two of them battling in their little house gives new meaning to cage fighting. I say, "But you already have two tattoos. Why is she so upset?"

"I don't know."

"What's the tattoo look like?"

"It's red roses under a sentence."

"What's the sentence?"

"ONLY GOD CAN JUDGE ME."

I can't help but laugh. "This is ironic. Doesn't Mom realize she's judging you?"

"It's not funny. Do something."

"I'm on it." I hang up and speed-dial my mother. When she answers, I cut the small talk. "Mom, he's 51 years old. If he wants a tattoo, he can have a tattoo."

"It's ugly."

"So what? He's upset."

"So am I."

"Why can't you just let it go?"

"No."

"But it's ironic, isn't it? I mean, his tattoo should say, ONLY MOM CAN JUDGE ME."

"I don't get it."

I don't explain. Evidently, irony doesn't come easily to The Flying Scottolines. We're too literal, or maybe insane.

Mother continues, "I don't know why your brother has to be this way. What's the matter with him? What did I do to deserve this? Why is he like this? Was he born this way?" She then throws the kind of fit that other parents throw when they find out their kid is gay. But that, she had no problem with.

Ironic, no?

She was fine with it from day one, when Frank told us that his friend Arthur was really his boyfriend. She even invited Arthur to move in with us, and she was happy to make extra meatballs for dinner. Now Arthur is gone and she lives with Frank in South Beach, where the two of them have a social circle of moms, gay sons, and meatballs. Their house smells like gravy and aftershave.

"Mom, you have to make up with him. Francesca's graduation is coming up."

"I won't speak to him there, either."

"You have to. You'll be sitting with him."

"No. You sit between us."

I try to argue with her, but I get nowhere. When my mother sets her jaw, she's an Italian Mount Rushmore. I cannot imagine them flying from Miami together, side-by-side, then going through the entire three days in Boston not speaking to each other.

Actually, I can, which is worse.

I have to prevent it, but I have only one weapon.

Guilt.

I choose my next words carefully. I don't want to give her a heart attack. My brother and I have been worried about giving my mother a heart attack ever since we woke her up too loudly and she told us we could give her a heart attack. I'm telling you now, if my mother gets a heart attack, it's my fault.

"Mom, think about it this way. None of us knows what will happen in life. What if something happened to you, or Frank?"

(By the way, I say this as if these two events are equally likely. To suggest otherwise would be tactless. Also I didn't want to give her a heart attack.)

"Mom, do you want your son's last memory to be that you wouldn't speak to him? Or your last memory of him to be that you wouldn't give him a kiss?"

"God forbid."

"Exactly."

"Make the call."

She hung up. She was already on it.

And the last I heard, they were having meatballs.

COMMENCEMENT DAY

Recently I had the great thrill of receiving an honorary degree, so I stayed up all night before, drafting a speech for commencement day. I tried to write something meaningful and profound, because you can't joke around in a commencement speech. It calls for loftier sentiments, and though I'm not incapable of same, I love to get laughs.

I was aiming for meaningful laughs.

In other words, every draft came out terrible.

I was up until dawn, fussing over 1500 words, which is crazy. It should have been easy. I can sneeze 1500 words. But go-out-and-change-the-world stuff doesn't come naturally to me. I hate to put that kind of pressure on people. Why isn't it good enough to live a decent life? For me, it is. If I can parallel park, I'm doing good.

Also, I was getting bollixed up by the fact that I had heard J. K. Rowling deliver the best commencement speech ever, and she outsells me 8,376,373,838 books to one. So I was having a major case of performance anxiety by the morning, even after I had drafted a generic go-change-the-world speech. I went downstairs to make a pot of coffee and a white light bulb went off in my head.

Literally.

And not in a good way.

There was a white flash of light, but no idea came to me. I blinked again, and my eyes didn't seem to clear. All I could see were bright prisms of colors, like looking out of a kaleidoscope.

I covered one eye and then the other, but all I could see were fragmented rainbows. I thought I was imagining it and went to look in the mirror, where I saw my own eyes staring back from wacky shards of color.

I had become a Cubist painting.

It wasn't a good look, for a single girl.

I went back up to the computer, logged into WebMD, and read through my colorful prisms, learning the symptoms of the various eye diseases. I determined that I didn't have macular degeneration or a detached retina, but the kaleidoscopes weren't clearing. I remained calm because there weren't a lot of other choices. Forty-five colorful minutes later, I was considering driving to the emergency room, through what would undoubtedly look like a psychedelic tunnel.

But the whole time I was thinking, what if I went blind? If I had a choice, which sense would I give up?

Sight would not be my first choice, though I have come to meet many wonderful people who have coped so well with their blindness. I'm also partial to smelling things, like lilacs and spaghetti sauce, which I love, or dog breath, which I love even more. And I've gotten used to hearing things, though I'd give up the sense of taste in a minute. Then everything would taste like tofu, and I'd lose weight.

But seriously, what would it be like if something I had taken for granted, like my eyesight, was suddenly taken away?

I sat there in my very vibrant haze and realized that tons of people go through this hardship, every day. They get a diagnosis that takes their sight, or their hearing, or their very life.

Just like that.

And my eyes suddenly cleared. No joke. The prisms dropped away, leaving me with a clear view of my computer and a dull headache. In time I called a doctor and found out I had experienced an ocular migraine, which can be brought on by lack of sleep over a 1500-word speech. But the good news was that because of my ocular excitement, I knew which 1500 words to write.

I threw out the change-the-world draft and wrote instead that the graduates should live in the moment. That they don't know how many moments are allotted to them, in this, their one and only life. That all of the blessings of this earth — as well as their very senses and the regular beat of their heart — aren't guaranteed to anyone. That interviewers will ask them where they think they'll be in five years, but life isn't to be lived in five-year stretches.

Life is moments.

And smells, and tastes, and the sight of your daughter's face. Or the sound of a kitten's purr.

So the only time is now.

That they call it commencement day because it's the beginning of life after college. But the real truth is, every day of life is commencement day.

Every day is a new day in which we wake up and choose how to live. Whether it's to apply for a job or to ask somebody out on a date. Or buy a sweater or save for a car. Or sell your house and find a better one. Or fall in love. That we choose every action in every day of our lives.

And I told them, and myself, to rejoice in the first of this string of commencement days. We don't have to know what's next. We shouldn't think about next now. Be right where you are, in the present, in this moment.

Your moment. Just be. And see and hear and smell. Because we are all of us so very lucky to begin again, every day.

Happy Commencement Day today.

And tomorrow, too.

GYM DANDY

As I get older, I'm figuring out that the reason people talk about their ailments is that they're sharing useful medical information. At least, this is the rationalization that works best for me, because while conversations about cholesterol and lower back pain used to bore me to tears, now all I want to talk about is cholesterol and lower back pain.

In the interests of full disclosure, I should say that I don't have lower back pain, but I hope to someday, so I can be like everybody else and join the national conversation. I do, however, have high cholesterol, which is why I'm on Lipitor, and I'd be happy to tell you about that, should you ask. In the meantime, kindly permit this story on a different medical subject.

Here's what happened.

Daughter Francesca came home from college and suggested that we join a gym, which is exactly the problem with educating your child. They get dangerous new ideas. Be forewarned.

But I went along with it, thinking it would be fun. Now, you should know that I'm no slouch in the physical department. I walk the dogs two miles a day, ride Buddy the Pony twice a week, and swear by the South Beach Diet. To be honest, I thought I had maybe five pounds to lose. By the way, you may have heard about that study in which women were asked if they'd rather lose five pounds or gain five IQ points. You know which they chose?

The five pounds.

I would, too. In fact, I would kill to lose five pounds. I'm pretty sure it would be justifiable homicide, at least if I got a woman judge.

Anyway, to get to the point, Francesca and I checked out the gyms in the neighborhood, which was fun. She asked about trainers, and I asked about defibrillators.

It may not be a good idea to join a gym with your kid. You look for different things. She wants treadmills, and you want CPR.

She's trying to look hot, and you're trying not to die.

Long story short, we joined the gym that gave us three free sessions with a trainer, and then we went for our first session. We started by warming up on the elliptical machines, watching *Judge Judy* on the big TVs, and yapping away. Then we met our trainer, a manchild with biceps that could cut hard cheese. I liked him until he told us it was time for our "evaluation," which included me holding a white plastic gadget that measured my body fat.

You wanna know?

Thirty-one percent.

WHAT?

I stopped having fun immediately. There had to be some mistake. My weight was in reasonable control, at least according to my bathroom scale, which always gives me good reviews. And I've been strict on my diet, if you don't count the margaritas.

Thirty-one percent body fat?

How did that happen? And when?

I considered the implications. A third of me was fat. I wondered if it was the top third or the bottom. Answer: It's the middle, stupid.

I couldn't believe it. How can you be not-that-overweight and have thirty-one percent body fat?

I'm guessing this is because of my age, which is really unfair. Why do we have to pay so high a price for sneaking a piece of chocolate now and then? The punishment doesn't fit the crime. I was so bummed that if I'd been home, I would have gone straight to the refrigerator.

But I was at the gym, so I lifted every weight the trainer gave me. I yanked every rope, flopped around on every beach ball, and curled muscles I'd sooner have left straight. I did everything but claw my thighs off in public.

And, of course, I signed up in for ten more sessions, to begin after the free ones ended. I didn't care what it cost. If I could have done all ten sessions on the spot, I would have done that, too.

Of course, you know what happened next.

The next day I could barely walk, sit, or drive. It hurt to laugh and breathe. It did not hurt to eat. It never hurts to eat. Not until later.

I'm thinking that maybe I should have taken the extra five IQ points.

Then I could figure out how to lose five pounds without going to the gym.

Happy Birthday

It's the time of year when Mother Mary comes to visit, and drama follows.

This time it begins as soon as I picked her up at the airport. Brother Frank wasn't able to make the trip with her, so he had ordered a wheelchair to fetch her from the gate. She can walk, but he wanted to make sure she was able to find her way out of Concourse A, and I thought that was a good idea.

So I waited for her at the end of the concourse, expecting to see her emerge in the wheelchair, but no dice. Easily three hundred people walked by me on their way out of the concourse, all of them tan and superhot, which I have learned is the Miami Express. Finally, at the tail end of the photogenic horde came Mother Mary, all four feet eleven of her, in her oversized white South Beach T-shirt and white Capri pants. She walked very slowly, watching every step to make sure she, didn't fall, so her head was downcast, showing a gray-white whorl at her crown. Right behind her was an exasperated airlines employee, pushing an empty wheelchair.

I didn't understand. "Mom, why aren't you in the wheelchair?"

"What did you say?" She cupped a hand to her ear.

"The wheelchair, behind you."

"Huh?"

"Forget it." I gave her a hug, and she felt little and soft in my arms, like an octogenarian Elmo.

The guy from the airlines shrugged in his maroon jacket. "I told her I had the wheelchair for her, but she walked right past me. I guess she didn't hear."

I took mother's arm. "Ma, you wearing your hearing aid?"

"What?" she asked, but I saw that it was nestled like a plastic comma behind her ear.

"I didn't hear," she said.

The reason she's here is that she asked me what I wanted for my birthday, and I told her — a visit from her. So she was guilted into coming, which I'm not above. We had my favorite birthday dinner of takeout hardshell crabs, and by the time the birthday cake was lit up with candles, I asked myself The Question.

Let me explain.

Every birthday I secretly ask myself this question: what lesson have I learned this year? This is my version of the birthday wish, because my birthday wish never comes true. For example, for many years, my go-to birthday wish was not to get older.

See what I mean?

So instead, I try to figure out what I learned this year, because if I have to get older, at least I'll get wiser. I make lots of mistakes every year, so I try to pick the biggest one and learn a lesson. My biggest lessons, of course, came from Thing One and Thing Two. And though someday I might make the mistake of Thing Three, I'm pretty sure that with my new system in place, I'll stop before Thing Nine.

Usually the lessons I've learned are Oprahesque. For example, last birthday, I learned to Ask for What You Want. The birthday before that was Take More Risks. And before that was, Don't Say You're About to Ask a Dumb Question before You Ask a Dumb Question, Because They'll Find Out Soon Enough.

But this year, my birthday lesson was simpler:

Margaritas are Fun.

That's one you can take to the bank.

It might even be BREAKING NEWS..

I learned it at my birthday dinner, when daughter Francesca showed off her college education by making us the most superb margaritas ever, and three generations of Scottoline women got sloshed en famille. We played Frank Sinatra on the iPod while my mother told stories from her first job, in Woolworth's toy department, when she was seventeen. She still remembered the toys she sold, and it turns out that Kewpie dolls and windup cars were big at Christmas, 1940.

And Francesca remembered that when she was six, she threw a stuffed animal at my mother, but was lucky enough to miss. And I watched them laugh in the candlelight, with Sinatra singing in the background, and I was thinking about how lucky I was to have them, and wondering if Margaritas Are Fun was my only lesson this year.

Because by the end of visit, I had learned a better lesson.

As Long As You Can Walk By Yourself, Do.

UNBREAKABLE

Francesca looked up from her magazine, open on the kitchen island. "Mom, it says here you're supposed to change your razor every three uses. Did you know that?"

"No."

"How often do you change your razor?"

I thought a minute. "Every three uses."

She waited a minute.

"Okay, every month."

Her eyes flared an incredulous blue. "That means you're scraping a rusty blade along your skin."

"Yeah, so?"

"So that's gross."

"It's an armpit. It's born gross. Why, how often do you change your razor?"

"I use it four times, then I throw it away."

"Good. I raised you right."

An hour later, I was driving Mother Mary to the airport to go back to Miami when she told me she was still angry about her colander that had broken, a month ago.

"What happened?" I asked.

"I drained the spaghetti and all of a sudden, the leg snapped off. You believe that? I loved that colander. You remember that colander?"

I watched rain dot the windshield, thinking a minute. "If it's a colander I remember, it must be kind of old."

"Nah." Mother waved me off with an arthritic hand. "It was about fifty."

"The colander was *fifty* years old?" I looked over, astounded. "*I'm* fifty years old!"

"Wrong. You're fifty-three."

I let it go. "So the colander was fifty, and you're angry that it broke?"

"Yeah."

"Fifty years is a long time, Ma."

"So what? I paid good money for it, and I had to throw it out."

I tried to process it. "But how much could you have paid, back then? A dollar?"

"How do I know? You think I remember? Fifty years is a long time."

My point exactly, but I let that go, too. You know the question I really wanted to ask. "Ma, how often do you change your razor?"

"What razor?"

"You know, the razor you shave with in

267

the shower."

She blinked behind her bifocals. "I don't shave."

I didn't understand. "How can you not shave, like your armpits or your legs?"

"I don't have hair anymore."

I tried to hold the car steady. Luckily we were almost at the airport. "What happened to your hair?"

"It went away."

"What? It disappeared?"

"Yeah. It's gone."

I felt appalled. I had no idea. Was I going to lose all my leg hair, too? Nobody told me, which is why I'm telling you. I needed more information, for both of us. "When did it go?"

She shrugged.

"Was it recently?"

"I don't know and I don't care."

We both fell quiet a minute, and the only sound was the *thumpa thumpa* of the windshield wipers. I worried that I'd made her self-conscious.

"Well, was it before the colander broke or after?" I asked, and we both laughed.

We reached the airport, where I parked and walked her to the gate, having successfully convinced the ticket agent that she gets confused in airports and needed to be escorted. We stopped by the gift shop, where she got two puzzle books and a bottle of water. They sold only the large bottles, which she struggled to hold in her gnarled fingers. We made our way to the gate and took our seats, her with her bottle and books on her lap, waiting for the plane and watching the babies go by. We thought every one was cute, but none cuter than Francesca when she was little. This is a conversation I never tire of, and the only person I can have it with is my mother, who was the first one at the child's bassinet twenty-odd years ago.

I gave her a nudge. "Ma, you know, Francesca throws her razor away every four uses."

Mother frowned. "Why?"

"The magazine says you're supposed to, now. After three times."

"Throw away a perfectly good razor?"

"Yes. It gets dull."

"What magazine says that?"

"I don't know."

"I do. A crazy magazine."

I thought about that a minute. About being old enough that all your hair has fallen out and you can barely hold the water bottle and you need help just to find the plane because all the announcements are incomprehensible in both English and Spanish, and the airlines love to play musical gates. About the fact that she had lived through a Depression, a world war, and the death of each and every one of her eighteen brothers and sisters, which is not a misprint. She was the youngest of nineteen children, three of whom died of the flu during their childhood, right here in America. Leaving only her, the youngest.

And she is still here.

The sole survivor.

Strong and on her feet, with all of her marbles. She lives in a world that changed from colanders that never break to razors that get tossed after only a week. She expects things not to break because she has not, after all.

She alone remains.

Unbreakable.

Mirror, Mirror

There's things I won't spend money on and things I will. For example, I spend money on pretentious clothes for book tour, and that's fine with me. I earn the money and I never judge people's spending habits, especially my own.

I learned this lesson when I met a man who had spent several thousand dollars on toy trains. You couldn't pay me to spend money on toy trains, but that's me. I could see it made him happy, which makes absolute sense, because he's not me. Turns out that money can buy happiness, if it runs on a miniature track past tiny fake shrubbery, and who am I to judge? Now, when I buy shoes, I think, at least I'm not blowing money on little model boxcars, for God's sake.

That would be really stupid.

To return to topic, here's what I don't spend money on:

My skin.

I wash my face with a three-dollar jug of Cetaphil that I buy at Walgreen's. If I'm feeling fancy, which I never am, I buy whatever drugstore moisturizer they're marketing for old broads. You know the one. They call it age-defying or age-defining or some other euphemism, but we weren't born yesterday, and we all know what it is — the menopausal moisturizer.

I'm thinking that the world divides into two groups: women who buy their skin-care products at CVS and those who buy them at the mall, which is where today's adventure starts in earnest.

I'm with daughter Francesca, standing at one of the nicest makeup counters at the mall, which also has a skin care line. Oddly, for the past few years, I've been getting free samples of this skin care line sent to me in the mail. I have no idea who sends them to me, whether it's the department store, the Skin Care Gods, or someone who has seen me on the street and been secretly revolted by my skin. But they've been sending me these products for a long time, and I've been giving them to Francesca. She'd told me that she liked them, and if I cared enough I would have found out why, but it's probably the one conversation we didn't have, until I found myself on the paying side of the glistening counter, listening to a gorgeous salesgirl with the most perfect skin ever describe how they put diamond dust in the face wash.

"Did you say diamonds?" I asked. If I had a hearing aid, I would have checked the battery.

"Yes, the dust exfoliates the skin."

"With *diamonds?*"

"Yes, and you have to make sure you wash it all off, or your face will be sparkly."

"Like a stripper?" I asked, and Francesca added:

"The richest stripper in the world."

Then we listened to the rest of the pitch, and in five minutes, I felt myself mesmerized by the salesgirl, or maybe by her skin. Her pores shimmered like precious gems, never mind that she was twenty years old, which means that she wasn't a salesgirl, but a saleschild.

Then she showed us a toner, which I had always thought was something you put in your computer printer but was actually applied to the face after diamond-exfoliating, and she also helped me understand that I needed both a day cream and a night cream, though I had never before thought about face cream having a time limit, which shows what a complete rube I've been.

She asked, "Do you ladies have an eye cream?"

Francesca had the right answer, which was yes, but only because she had cheated and had gotten the free sample, which I must have been insane to give to her, as my eyes now clearly thirsted for their cream. I wondered if there were special creams for other things on your face, like lip or nose cream, but I was too spellbound to ask.

The saleschild turned again to me. "Which serum do you use?"

"Serum?" My mind flipped ahead to the possibilities. Truth serum? Serum cholesterol? Huh?

"There comes a time when every women needs a serum." The saleschild held up a tiny green bottle from which she extracted a medicine dropper. "Now, hold out your hand."

"Yes, master." I obeyed, and she let fall a perfect teardrop of serum onto the back of my hand, leaving a costly wet spot that dried sooner than you can say, Charge it!

"The infusion is absorbed instantly into the skin, leaving it revived and refreshed."

"Like a magic potion," I said, awed, when I felt Francesca's strong and sensible hand on my arm.

"Mom, we should go."

But I could only hear her as if from far away. I had slipped over to the dark side, and by the time we left the mall, I had a shopping bag full of bottles and tubes, jars and gels.

In other words, toy trains.

DISASTROUS

I don't know what kind of conversations you had around your dinner table growing up, but ours were generally about disasters. Mother Mary could make a disaster out of anything. Our kitchen was an accident waiting to happen. I reprint below her most important warnings, in case you're sitting in your breakfast nook, blissfully unaware.

If you put too much spaghetti on your fork, you'll choke to death. If you don't chew your spaghetti twenty times, you'll choke to death. If you talk while you're eating spaghetti, you'll choke to death. Bottom line, spaghetti leads to perdition.

Spaghetti isn't the only killer. If you load the knives into the dishwasher with the pointy tip up, you'll fall on them and impale yourself. Also you'll go blind from reading without enough light. Reading in general ruins your eyes. If you eat baked beans from a can that has dents, you'll die of botulism.

This was before people injected botulism into their faces. Nowadays, the dented can will kill you, but you'll look young.

You should know that electrocution, a go-to Scottoline hazard, will result from many common house hold items. You'll be electrocuted if you use the phone during a thunderstorm. If your nighttime glass of water spills onto your electric alarm clock, you'll fry in your sleep. In fact, any small electrical appliance, given the chance, will leap into the nearest sink to kill you. Trust me, blow dryers lie in wait. Your toaster has murder on its mind.

A closely related disaster is fire, and almost anything can start a five-alarmer. Birthday candles. Lightning striking the house or the car. The stove left on. A cigarette butt tossed unpinched into the trash. Oddly, nobody in my house worried about smoking. If you smoke, you'll be fine.

Exercise is lethal. If you play a sport, the ball will hit you in the breasts, presumably deflating them. You're a goner if you run with scissors or sharpened pencils. Swimming less than an hour after you eat is out of the question, but if you want to play it safe, better to wait until tomorrow. And if you don't listen and sink like a stone, don't come crying to me.

It's your funeral.

As a result of my valuable childhood preparedness training, I'm the lady stockpiling milk, eggs, bread, rock salt, and snow shovels before a storm. And during the anthrax scare, I was first in line at the hardware store. I bought the requisite cord of Saran Wrap and a gross of duct tape, with which to seal the house, and all of it sits in my basement, at the ready. The deadly cloud of anthrax never came, and for that you have me to thank. I pre-empted it. I scared anthrax. I had enough Saran Wrap to protect all of us, if not keep us fresh for days.

Now that you know how prepared I am, you can imagine my dismay when I read something recently reiterating that all manner of disasters could happen — wildfires, hurricanes, and tornados — and I should go online to test my "readiness quotient" (RQ).

Uh-oh.

I'm terrified to report that even though I unplug my blow dryer after each use and load my knives correctly, my RQ score was a 0 out of 10.

I knew I should have studied.

The report said that the average RQ score for Americans is 4, and that only two other people in my zip code had taken the test.

Here's where I went wrong, so you can learn from my mistakes:

Not only did I not know how to find the emergency broadcast system on my radio, I couldn't even find my radio.

I don't have a disaster supply kit, and duct tape doesn't count.

I don't have a "Go" kit. I have only a "Stay Home And Wait It Out" kit.

I don't have a "family communications plan." Honestly, who does? Communications are hard enough, but family communications are impossible. You have a better chance of surviving a tornado than communicating with your family.

In event of a disaster, I haven't established a specific meeting place, but that's easy to choose. The mall.

I don't drill my family on what to do in an emergency. Scream Hysterically was not an option. Nor was Hurry Back To The Mall.

Nor do I know first aid. Evidently, a box of assorted Band-Aids, even the kind with the antibiotic, isn't enough. This surprises me. When the earthquake hits, my money's on Neosporin.

So you know where this is going. I suggest you log on to www.whatsyourrq.org, test yourself, and get your act together before the apocalypse.

See you at the hardware store. I'll be the one in the gas mask.

In a gas mask, I look young.

Dog Days

Because I lectured you in my commencement speech to slow down and savor the moments of your life, I thought you should know I'm doing nothing like that.

I flunk savoring.

I know it's the drowsy dog days of summer and I'm supposed to enjoy sitting around watching the tomatoes ripen and noticing the particular hue of the sunlight as it hits the leafy trees and blah blah blah. Summer sounds like literary fiction, but I write books with car chases.

In other words, I got a new summer project.

Let's see if you can guess what it is. It involves wood, nails, and feathers.

Give up?

A chicken coop.

With chickens.

Here's how it happened. You know how I am about home decorating, and I just finished with the house, to mixed results. The good news is that the aluminum siding is gone, the stonework looks fantastic, and the clapboard is fresh Bavarian Cream.

The bad news is that the shutters are painted a bright yellow called Candleglow, which is a misnomer. This color is Solar Energy. This color could power a small city. A tactful friend of mine called it "sunny," but sunny doesn't come close. If you broke off a piece of the sun itself and stuck it on either side of your windows, you would still only have half of this color. Now you need sunglasses to look at my house, and when you do, you understand instantly why yellow was Vincent Van Gogh's favorite color.

Because he was crazy.

Look at my shutters and you not only want to cut your ears off, you want to gouge your eyes out. But you couldn't, because you'd be blinded by the color. Your face might even melt off, too. It's like Atomic Blast Yellow, and you get the idea. It's a man-made disaster.

Correction. Woman-made, even better.

I'm trying to live with it, until I get the money to repaint or detonate.

To return to my point, fresh from my success with the house, I saw a picture of a chicken coop. It was adorable, like a doll-house with a little wooden door and two tiny windows, with shutters. It reminded me of the Little Tykes playhouse that daughter Francesca used to have when she was little, or those green plastic houses in Monopoly that you put on Baltic Avenue. I always preferred the houses over the hotels, even though the hotels earned more rent, which gives you an idea of my money management skills.

Anyway when I saw the picture of the coop, I said to myself, I want that little housie, so I guess I have to get some chickens. So now we know which came first, the chicken or the coop.

As it happens, this summer project is fun for everyone in my family, meaning Francesca and me. We went and picked out seven adorable chicks, and we learned new vocabulary words — Brown Sussex, Wyandotte, Araucana, and Australorp, which is a black chicken and not a resident of Australia. They're all pullets, which means girls, so it took us days to pick their names because we wanted a theme. First we went with Miss Pennsylvania, Miss New Jersey, Miss Delaware, and so on, but they peep like crazy so we tried Sheryl Crow, Alanis Morrisette, Barbra Streisand, and Judy Garland. Then we couldn't agree on seven girl rock stars, which is clearly what these chicks are, so we decided the dominant one should be Princess Ida and the rest are all other characters from Gilbert & Sullivan, which classes up my house.

We hang with the chicks all the time, watching them grow, singing to them, and trying to get them to love us. The first week they fled from us in fear, flocking at the corner of the cage, but now they're eating out of our hands, literally. They coo, cluck, and gurgle, and today I'm going out to buy a baby monitor so I can hear them in the house. I'm sure this has nothing to do with Francesca's graduation from college and undeniable adulthood, but call the police if I try to nurse these chicks.

Ouch.

We obsess on raising and lowering their heat lamp, and we clean their butts, called "vents," with mineral oil so they don't "paste up" or, well you guessed it. We also talk about painting the chicken coop pink, since it was an all-girl production, or drawing fake flowers and vines on it, because why not, then considered painting it like a sorority house with Greek letters above the door, or maybe a little theater, since the chicks are all Drama Queens.

So I'm back to paint chips and shutter colors.

I'm thinking Egg Yolk Yellow.

WHAT I DID ON SUMMER VACATION

I had originally decided that daughter Francesca and I would skip a vacation this year in favor of a staycation, but that was before I realized how much I hated saying staycation, which isn't even a word. So I grabbed my VISA card and made a few phone calls, and we were off to a place no Scottoline has ever been.

Hawaii.

The excitement started before we even got there, because of Michael McDonald. Please tell me you know that Michael McDonald sang with the Doobie Brothers and Steely Dan, who made the soundtrack of your life, or at least your freshman year at the University of Pennsylvania, circa 1974. I spotted him in the airport, recognizing him instantly from my fantasies. You know you're getting older when the grayest head in the place is the one man who does it for you.

Of course, I made Francesca go over to

him with me, which she did, and I introduced myself and started gushing, though
she pulled me away before I suggested
anything untoward.

Who raised this kid?

So then of course I have the best luck ever
and Michael McDonald shows up on our
very flight, which lasts like 29,373 hours so
I can stare at him as he watches the movie
(*Prince Caspian*) and gets up to go to the
bathroom (only three times).

I like a man with a strong bladder.

And then how great is it that when we get
our baggage, the only luggage left is his and
mine, which shows that we were meant to
be, if you don't factor in his wife.

What a fool believes, a wise woman has
the power to reason away.

And then Francesca and I end up on
Maui, which is ridiculously pretty, if only I
could enjoy it. Because all I like to do on
vacation is sit on my butt and read in the
sun, which is what distinguishes a vacation
from a staycation, wherein I sit on my butt
and read in the sun for much less money.

But Maui offers so much to do and Francesca is the adventurous sort, so in no time,
I find myself snorkeling in its teal blue
water, watching green-striped eels and spotted manta rays. By the way, I can't swim, a

fun fact about me you may not know. So I'm the only adult in the Pacific wearing an inflatable vest.

Six-year-olds point and laugh.

At one point, I have to struggle out of the water to shore, so I do my best doggy paddle while Francesca waits on the beach for me. She tries to be patient but by sundown, it gets old. She says, "Dead bodies wash up faster."

I cannot disagree. Glug.

Then we sign up for the snorkeling cruise, which means that we spend two hours on a catamaran sailing to the island of Lanai. In case you don't know, a catamaran is a two-hulled boat that causes you to throw up, which I do.

The next day we are scheduled for a horseback ride down the crater of Haleakala. FYI, Haleakala is a dormant volcano that rises 10,000 feet into the air, and another fun fact about me is that I'm afraid of heights. I'm too terrified to drive the road to the summit, which snakes along various lethal cliffs, so I pay an extortionate rate to be driven there, only to realize that I cannot pay anyone to ride the horse down into the crater for me. So I suck it up for the next five hours, over trails that go up and down for three thousand feet, over lava rubble and coarse sand. Francesca tells me it was starkly beautiful — a rust, black, and green landscape that looks like Mars, dotted with unusual silver sword plants that grow only in Hawaii — and I'm taking her word for it.

My eyes were closed.

I survived only by placing my trust in my sleepy old mare, who can do Haleakala with her eyes closed, just like me. Her name is Princess, so there's something else we have in common.

Much later, back at the hotel, I order drinks that are also found only on Hawaii. The Lavaflow, a pina colada with strawberries, and a perfect Mai-Tai, and the next day I am sitting happily on the beach, reading James Michener's *Hawaii.*

Now that's a vacation.

Shake It Up, Baby

Okay, I'm officially confused, and it's not rocket science. It's about my latest trip to the food store.

Here's what happened:

I shop at Acme and Whole Foods, because I can't buy everything I need in one place. Acme doesn't know from wheatberry salad, and God forbid that Whole Foods sell Splenda. I even have to go to a third store for pet food, but that's not the point.

Back to Whole Foods.

We all know it sells hippie food at designer prices, but I love it for all its crazy and delicious choices. Also, the samples are incredible. Whenever you're hungry, you should go directly to Whole Foods, walk around, and eat anything attached to a toothpick. Better yet, grab five and put them in your pocket.

The cheese cubes travel better than the chicken quesadillas.

But to stay on point, Whole Foods has every fruit possible in its produce department, where you can choose from organic or "conventional." I always buy conventional because I am conventional. Also it's cheaper, and I like my apples pretty. If they sold plastic apples, I'd be happier, but either way, I appreciate Whole Foods for its euphemistic "conventional." They could have called it "for people who cheap out on their family" or "for people who choose style over substance" or "for people who think a little DDT never hurt anybody."

But they didn't.

So I went to Whole Foods with my shopping list and was happily collecting mangoes and multigrains when I came upon an endcap that showed an array of mysterious plastic tubs, each larger-than-life. The labels read: whey protein powder in natural vanilla flavor and whey protein powder in natural chocolate favor.

I blinked, bewildered. The only whey I'd ever heard of came with curds and a spider.

Next to the whey powder were big vats of soy protein powder, also in chocolate and vanilla, then next to that were tubs of Green Superfood Berry Flavored Drink Powder and Green Superfood Chocolate Drink Powder, made with "organic green foods."

All of the powder tubs came with a 28-ounce "BlenderBottle," like a sippy cup for grown-ups.

It was dizzying. They were clearly some kind of meal replacement, so I was looking at a wallful of drinkable food. Just add water. That's my favorite kind of cooking.

I spent the next hour squinting at the labels, comparing the nutrition facts and deciphering the language, such as "includes Free-Form Branch Chain Amino Acids." Now, I don't know about you, but when I want to cheat on my diet, I head straight for the amino acids. Especially if they're from the branch and not the main office. Which is so not free-form.

There was even a big white tub of Mega-Food, which immediately got my attention. If I were going to put any prefix in front of the word "food," it would be "mega." Except, of course, for pizza. I looked but couldn't find any MegaPizzaFood, which would have made my day.

I bet Acme has it. Next to the Splenda.

Instead I had to settle for the DailyFoods Organic Greens Dietary Supplement, which billed itself as "revitalizing greens for women over 40." It promised "detoxification," but I wondered how I became toxic. Was it merely the act of turning forty and being a woman? Or maybe it was those frozen margaritas over vacation. Or that time I ate all the Snickers out of my daughter's Halloween candy. Which happened for the entire ten years she went out for Halloween.

Amazingly, the tub of girl powder had vitamin A, vitamin C, and vitamin K, which I didn't even know existed. It also had riboflavin, niacin, folic acid, and 19mg of chlorophyll, which is the powder equivalent of eating your shrubbery.

Plus it had "Anti-Aging SuperFoods," and I'm so there. If there's anything I'm anti, it's aging, especially as applied to me. I'm also anti-dying, but not even Whole Foods sells that stuff.

Or if they do, it's really really really expensive.

Bottom line, even I could figure out that the powders were packed with more protein, vitamins, and minerals than anything I had in my shopping cart. I looked at the shiny tubs of powder, then I looked at my lame cart of old-fashioned broccoli, pears, and lettuce. Suddenly, it looked so terribly . . . conventional.

How had I come to the food store and bought all the wrong things — food?

Obviously, anything in the tubs was superior to the groceries in my cart. For starters, all the stuff in the tubs was one word, with capitals even — FoodState, SuperFood, DailyFoods. How can a lower-case banana compete? And broccoli doesn't come with a BlenderBottle.

So I'm confused.

If you could make all food taste like chocolate, why wouldn't you?

And why have a meal, when you can have a meal replacement? You can throw away all your silverware — and your teeth.

And who wants dumb, old-fashioned peas when you could have powder with "Cold Fusion FoodState Nutrients"? This is food that splits the atom, people. Or maybe fuses it together. I don't know, I always forget what cold fusion is. Clearly, this food is way smarter than I am.

Maybe it is rocket science, after all.

EGGISTENTIAL

I have a problem to solve, and I'm talking about something really hard, like programming a VCR, or marriage.

I'm talking about what to eat.

Here's what happened.

I used to eat everything, including red meat. Hamburgers, steaks, the whole thing. I loved rare roast beef with extra Russian dressing, which I used to order at a place called the Corned Beef Academy. That's how much of a meat eater I was. Even my restaurants were carnivorous.

But then daughter Francesca was born and we started going to a petting zoo that had the cutest calf in the world. Brown eyes like melted Hershey's Kisses, and a spongy nose as pink as the inside of a conch shell. In no time, I'm naming the calf and visiting it way more than anyone should. Francesca lost interest, but I didn't, and after a time, I felt too guilty to eat red meat. Don't get me wrong. It wasn't an ethical thing. I just couldn't take the guilt.

Then years later, I saw the movie *Babe,* starring a baby piglet. I know that was only a story, but I saw that Hollywood piglet do everything the fictional piglet was supposed to do, so I started feeling too guilty to eat pork chops and bacon. You have to be crazy to quit eating bacon. Bacon is the meth of meats.

And to be clear: If you eat meat, I don't judge you, I envy you. I want to be you again. I don't know what to eat anymore, because it gets worse:

As you know, I have these chicks. They need a special fence with a top to protect them from hawks and stuff, so until the fence gets built, I sit and watch over them like a chicken security guard. In other words, I get no work done and spend way too much time watching them, and you know where this is going.

Now I can't eat chicken.

First off, they're all cute and little, like cartoon chicks. You remember Sylvester and Tweety Bird. I Taw a Putty Tat! How can I eat Tweety Bird? Even with fresh rosemary?

Plus, they do cute things. They make adorable peeps and coos. When they drink water, they throw their heads back like they're gargling. They run around gathering tiny twigs and running back inside the coop with them, like me after a sale at Neiman Marcus.

And each chick has a different personality; Buttercup is a show-off, Yum-Yum bosses everyone around, and Josephine never shuts up.

They're women, remember?

The Bard Rocks, the black-and-white chicks who make up the chorus, love to be held. They're soft as a pillow in the crook of my arm, and their little feet are warm with blood. They even stay still while I kiss them, and I've become a big-time chicken kisser.

I try not to touch their breasts.

That would be weird.

So now I can't eat red meat or chicken. I even look at eggs funny. Is a yolk a future Yum-Yum? Or is it just yummy?

When does chick life begin? It's not an existential problem. It's an eggsistential problem.

Remember, I'm not preaching at you, because I'm not even morally consistent. My car has leather seats, and I own a leather jacket. I buy leather shoes by the boatload. As long as I don't eat them, I don't feel guilty.

Meantime, all I can eat is pasta, bread,

and oatmeal. I went from a no-carb diet to an all-carb diet, all because of guilt. I've gained five pounds, and now I feel guilty about that.

And tofu isn't the answer because I've done everything possible with tofu, which means drown it in something with flavor. I rotate teriyaki sauce, soy and ginger sauce, and even tomato sauce, which could cause me to forfeit my Italian-American credentials, should it come to light.

I make protein shakes like they're going out of style, and now I'm even getting sick of chocolate.

What's the matter with me? How can I change it? What should I do?

All I know is one thing:

I'm not getting a goldfish.

WILLING

I'm making out my will, and, as you can imagine, I'm having the time of my life.

Or death.

It's a laugh riot to contemplate your own demise. Not that it takes a will for me to do it. As you know, my mother taught me that I can perish at any moment, especially if I stand near a toaster during a thunderstorm. But I never had to make so many decisions, all of which involve things that take place after I'm dead. You'd think that at some point, I'd get to stop worrying, but no. Evidently, death isn't all it's cracked up to be. I bet my skin doesn't even clear up.

But I look on the bright side. If I had died when I was a struggling writer, I'd have nothing to leave but three maxed-out credit cards and a very hungry dog.

Bottom line, now I have to decide who gets the do-re-mi when I'm gone, which is easy. I have only daughter Francesca, and she's cashing in. I told her this morning, and already she's looking at me funny.

I'm locking up the steak knives.

I'm telling you now, if something happens to me, we all know who did it. She's smart enough to make it look like an accident, so don't believe a word. She went to Harvard, remember?

But who inherits is only one of the decisions I have to make. A harder question is raised by the living will, as opposed to the dying will, I guess. You know what a living will is; it's a piece of paper that says what you want to happen if you're completely incapacitated, like me after a head injury or two Cosmopolitans. The main question is do I want the plug pulled? I say no.

"You're kidding, right?" my lawyer asks, over the phone.

"No. In fact, I want that plug duct-taped into the socket, so it doesn't get kicked out by accident on purpose. And while you're at it, get me an extension cord, a surge protector, and a generator, right by my bed. Just in case. And padlock it. Did I mention that my kid went to Harvard?"

"You mean that you want your daughter to visit you for years and years, even though you're in a coma?"

"Yes. Years and years and years, even

though I'm in a coma. You never know. I'm a light sleeper."

The lawyer doesn't laugh. "But that's such a burden on her."

"Aw, poor wittle thing. Where was she when I was in labor? Oh, that's right. Being born."

The lawyer gives up and we move on to the hardest decision of all:

The Anatomical Gift.

I see that phrase in the will and immediately I'm thinking, George Clooney. I bet he has an Anatomical Gift. And if he gave it to me, I'd die and go to heaven.

But the lawyer explains that the Anatomical Gift refers to my anatomy, which I may decide to give away after I'm dead. Plus I have to specify any "organs or body parts."

Now I have a question for all of you:

Who wants my cellulite?

This is grade-A quality cellulite, and you can't beat the price. Send me an email, write me an essay, fifty words or less.

Anybody else want my nose?

It's big. Really big. My mother says I get more oxygen than anybody else in the room.

At least I did, when I was breathing.

So let me know. Yours for the asking.

But the lawyer gets me back to business. The last question is, do I want to be an organ donor "for transplantation or for medical research?"

This gives me pause. "I don't want anybody pointing and laughing at my cellulite, in case nobody writes a good enough essay."

"Please answer."

"Okay, yes." Then I get a load of the final provision in the draft will: Treatment which prolongs my dying may be temporarily continued or modified so as to preserve and protect for transplant the useful portions of my body.

Okay to that, too, but if they want my kidneys, they can make it snappy.

And trust me, my ovaries rock.

Step lively.

EXIT STRATEGIES FOR WOMEN AND CHICKENS

Everybody asks me what daughter Francesca is doing now that she's graduated from college. So I thought I'd let her tell you herself, because it's something that your kids might be dealing with, too:

At some point in every young adult's life, she has to make the most illogical decision of her life: to move out.

Moving out makes no sense. If we young people gave this any real thought, we would see that it's a terrible idea. Take me, for instance. I've been living at home since I graduated from college this past spring, and I'm starting to feel that itch to move out. But the more I think about it, the more nonsensical it seems. In the rare moments when I have some objectivity, and I catch myself rolling an eye or huffing a melodramatic sigh, I have to ask myself, what do I have to complain about, *really?*

It's awfully quiet here in the burbs. But am I so easily dissatisfied that I'm knocking a place because it's too idyllic? There has to be something else. Living with my mom can be annoying. But, let's be fair, I can be annoying. Occasionally annoying each other is the hallmark of a healthy mother-daughter relationship. Most of the time we get along pretty great, and don't tell her, but I missed her when I was at school. A lot.

So what am I doing navigating back to Craigslist.com, refreshing my list of New York City apartments, "cozy" at five hundred square feet and "A STEAL" at an extortionate $2500 a month? I live in a house, for FREE, with my own bedroom and bathroom, and a washer-dryer — not down the street, but *down the hall* — and, oh boy, do we allow pets. Have I lost my mind? Is anyone with this kind of judgment even capable of taking care of herself in the real world? Why would I leave this?

It's home.

And the psychology of the thing is topsy-turvy. For instance, you might have read the above paragraphs and thought to yourself, "Atta girl. She's starting to appreciate what she's got, now that's maturity." That's the nutty part; as soon as I am mature enough to realize how good I have it at home, that means I am ready to move out. But then I start not wanting to! And if I start appreciating home too much, you'll start to worry that I may never leave, so then I really have to get out of here, pronto!

I don't blame you; I worry about me, too. For a twenty-two-year-old single gal, it's scary how easily I can slip into home life. I complain to my friends about how dull it is, but secretly, I'm not bored at all. I have been far more bored by frat boys, flip cup, and other elements of "exciting" college life. In a way, I love this quiet life. I could live here forever.

Oh my God, what am I saying? I have to move out!

See what I mean?

Now, on the other hand, if I recognize that I am at risk of becoming a total mooch, and I should get out there and live on my own, well, then I have proven my maturity and I am free to take my time finding a place. So basically, when I want to move out, I don't have to. But when I don't want to move out, that means I have to — and fast!

A most ingenious paradox.

But what does it all mean? How can I make sense out of my illogical, nonsensical, paradoxical desire to move out?

Believe it or not, a little birdie told me.

We lost one of our little chickens the other day. In fact, she is the very littlest of our flock, "Peep-Bo," a small Brown Sussex, who only just got her adult feathers and who mostly sticks with her twin sister and avoids being picked up. Somehow, she escaped from the fence and decided to bolt for the forest. She disappeared into the thorny brush, her speckled brown feathers blending perfectly into the fallen leaves. My mom and I tried looking for her for four hours, until darkness fell, and we went home devastated and covered in mud and scratches. That night there was a thunderstorm, and all I could think about was how poor little Peep-Bo was outside, all alone, away from her sisters and her warm, dry house.

The next day, thankfully, Peep-Bo was spotted marching around the woods, and after a comical chase, my mom and I were able to catch her and bring her home.

So why did the chicken fly the coop?

Just to see if she could.

PASSWORD

In the beginning, God created the Internet and shopping online. I was an early believer. Where shopping is involved, I get in on the ground floor, especially if I don't have to move from my chair. Shopping online was like having somebody bring you brownies and stuff them in your mouth.

In other words, impossible to resist.

Plus the economy was better then. It turns out that "shop until you drop" wasn't such a hot idea. Or maybe we just dropped. Or somebody dropped us. Either way, don't get me started.

To stay on point, early on, websites like Amazon and bn.com required a four-digit password. It was my first password, and what a thrill! Think of a secret word! It put me in mind of decoder rings, speakeasies, and people knocking on doors, saying "Sam sent me." In those days, I used the same go-to password for everything — specifically, my goal weight plus zero. It was easy to remember because nobody ever forgets their goal weight, and the chance of ever attaining it is zero.

Then everybody caught on to online shopping, so much so that the other day I went into a pet store and they had only two dog collars, both large and blue. I wanted red and small, so they told me go home and shop online at their website. So you know where this is going. The bad news is that someday the stores will be empty. The good news is that there'll be plenty of parking.

But somewhere along the line, passwords stopped being fun. Complex rules entered the picture, like an IRS Code for passwords. Nowadays passwords have to be eight or ten digits, mix numbers and letters, use both upper and lowercase, no asterisks or other punctuation, can't repeat digits, and never on Sunday.

Now I hate passwords.

I have 3,929,874 passwords, not only for shopping but for banking, Gmail, satellite radio, and other stuff. I try to keep track of them but I can never remember to record the password, and if I keep forgetting it, I get locked out of the website and have to reset the password. Then I reset the password to something close to the original, which means that all of my passwords are scarily similar, like some inbred mountain family, so I'll never be able to keep them straight.

And then websites started requiring user names, because our regular names stopped being good enough and we became users and not people. I can never remember my user names, because sometimes the website requires lscottoline or lisascottoline or lisa@scottoline.com, and the other day I got so fed up, I made "password" my user name.

This amused me.

Then of course I couldn't get into a website because I misremembered either my user name or my password, and they don't tell you which one you got wrong, so you have to try different combinations to hit paydirt, which never happens before you are locked out of the site. And you can't get an email sent to you reminding you of your password unless you remember your user name. But if you're like me and you forgot your password, you're also the type to forget your user name, which is when you throw your laptop out the window.

But it gets better.

Yes, I'm talking about Security Questions. These are something my bank has come up with, wherein after I finally get my user name and password correct, they ask me questions, the answers to which I established too long ago to remember, around the time I lost my car keys. And if I get all the answers right, I'm still not in the clear, because the website shows me a picture of an oak tree and asks me to remember the caption I wrote for the picture, once upon a time.

Huh?

I can write a novel, but not a caption. All my captions stink. And so therefore they're impossible to remember.

I look at the oak tree picture and try the caption, "This is an oak tree."

Incorrect.

Then I try, "This is not an oak tree."

Surreal, but also incorrect.

I try "Oaky Dokey!" For fun.

Also incorrect, so I'm locked out of the bank. At which point, I leave the house to go to the store.

And park.

Coo Coo Ca Choo

Let us now discuss cougars. Not the "large, tawny cat" defined by dictionary.com, but women over forty who date younger men. In other words, not the feline, but the female.

You used to be able to find cougars in the mountains, but now cougars are online in their bra and undies, at www.dateacougar .com, which invites younger men to log on to meet "Older Beautiful Women" in the "cougar community."

I'm trying to figure out how I feel about cougars.

I get it, in principle. Older men have been dating younger women since the dawn of time, and usually I think turnabout is fair play. What's good for the goose is good for the gander, though I keep forgetting which is the girl. Maybe it's time for men to see what it feels like when the stiletto is on the other foot.

Although please note that when an older woman dates a younger man, she's called a predator. When an older man dates a younger woman, he's called a success.

But still, what is going on here? Do these men want mothers? Can anyone really want a second mother? You could die from guilt of that magnitude.

And do these women really feel younger when they're the one with all the wrinkles? I like my men even wrinklier than me. If I could date a prune, I would.

But let's look to history for guidance.

Probably the first recorded cougar was Mrs. Robinson, the wealthy housewife who preyed on Dustin Hoffman in *The Graduate*. She had great eyeliner, but boozed it up, seduced her daughter's boyfriend, and wore leopard, the hallmark of cougardom. Ironically, cougar is not the fur of choice for cougars. Don't ask me why. I'm new around here.

Other old-school cougars were equally drunk, or worse, overly made-up. Think Mrs. Dubcek in *3rd Rock From the Sun,* if you can follow my literary references. She was the landlord on the show, who smoked, drank, and flirted, the cougar trifecta.

Then Demi Moore came along, not only

dating Ashton Kutcher but marrying him, and it was a turning point in cougar history. Demi brought respectability to cougars everywhere. She could have had any man she wanted, but she chose a man-child.

Demi taught us that you don't have to be drunk to realize that Ashton Kutcher is drop-dead gorgeous. And maybe smart and a nice guy, too, but who cares. He's super-hot, and if he needs a little help with his French homework, so much the better.

Nowadays, cougars abound. Hollywood types like Halle Berry, Kristin Chenoweth, and Drew Barrymore all date younger men. Every day I meet normal women who date younger men, and none of them dies from exertion.

Hmm.

I confess I almost have some experience in this area.

A near-miss.

Once upon a time, I met a very nice young man. He was twenty-something to my forty-something, and even more gorgeous than Ashton Kutcher, and I wasn't drunk at the time. When he asked me out, I thought I'd heard him wrong. After all, I was doddering to his toddling.

Usually I have better self-esteem, but all I could think was, why do you want to go out with me, child? I'm old enough to be your mother. And if I were, I'm pretty sure I would have nursed you.

Heh heh.

In any event, this happened before cougar nation, so I didn't take him seriously. I forget what I said, but I think it was something cringeworthy like, "You must be joking."

Ouch.

In those days, it didn't seem like it would be okay to go out with a man half my age. I thought people would laugh at me, or him. Plus I couldn't see myself with someone who didn't know Steely Dan. And my days of pushing a stroller were over, though he would have looked so cute in OshKosh B'Gosh overalls.

But now, times have changed, and I have to ask myself, do I regret saying no?

You bet your ass I do.

I mean, perhaps.

Maybe cougars are a good thing, after all. I'm suspicious of men who go out with much younger women, because I think they need to be adored. So what's the matter if women need to be adored, too? I mean, so what if he doesn't know Steely Dan?

So I've been wrong. Go for it, ladies. I don't judge you.

Find the right guy, and teach him a thing or two.

THANKFUL

Thanksgiving is just around the corner, which means that we're all crazy busy, me included. I'm busy thinking about when to pick up daughter Francesca from the train and how to smuggle her puppy onto Amtrak, then I'm deciding whether to make a turkey or tofu shaped like a turkey, and finally I have to go hunting for fresh cranberries, so I don't have to serve canned sauce with its telltale dents. And with the rest of the holidays approaching, like everybody else, I'm busy worrying about the economy. Every day the news reports more layoffs and downturns, and that worries me more than canned cranberries. Banks and car companies get bailouts because they're big, but none of us do, because we're little.

It seems backwards.

Anyway my head was full of these thoughts the other afternoon, as I was hurrying in a downpour through the streets of New York

City, there to take my author photo. I know that sounds glamorous, and it would be if I were ten pounds lighter and ten years younger, but take it from me, the best fiction in my books is the author photo.

But that's not my point.

My point is that I was running down the street in a city I don't know, with no umbrella in the pouring rain, thinking about Thanksgiving and the economy and so preoccupied that I couldn't find the photographer's studio, which was at number 98. I ran back and forth between numbers 96 and 100 and then between 94 and 102, but I couldn't find 98 and I was drenched and late. Throngs of people hurried past me on the street, their umbrellas slanted against the rain, and just when I was about to freak, a voice behind me said:

"You look lost. Can I help you?"

I turned around, and standing there was an older man holding an umbrella and wearing a suit and tie. His hooded eyes looked genuinely concerned, so I answered: "I can't find number 98."

"Take my umbrella, and I'll look."

And before I could object, he put his umbrella in my hand, hustled off down the sidewalk, and disappeared into the crowd. He came back five minutes later, pointing.

"It's three doors down, out of order, after the loading dock."

"Really?"

"Come, I'll show you," he said, guiding me to a glass building that read number 98, where I gave him back his umbrella.

"Thanks so much."

"No problem, take care," he said with a quick smile, and in the next second he joined the throng of umbrellas hurrying down the street.

Leaving me in the middle of the sidewalk, suddenly not minding the rain and feeling a warm rush of gratitude. For the first time in a long time, I stopped worrying about Thanksgiving and started feeling thankful.

And not thankful for the usual things, like good health and a lovely child. Not even thankful to the usual people, like my family and friends. Those people, I thank all the time. But this time, I felt thankful for a complete and total stranger, who went out of his way to help me.

In fact, I realized, I had gotten bailed out, after all.

And it wasn't money that bailed me out, it was better than money. It was time, concern, and human kindness.

It reminded me of other people who have gone out of their way to bail me out, and I suddenly felt thankful for them, too. Because while it's easy to look around and wonder why I'm not getting something that someone else gets, that encounter reminded me to be thankful for the many bailouts that come my way. I can recount them now, but I won't. They'll be part of my silent prayer of thanks over the turkey and/or tofu served with canned and/or fresh cranberry sauce, sitting with my lovely daughter across a dining room table, and sleeping underneath, several overweight dogs and one very tired puppy.

But you should know, right now, that among the people who bail me out are the people who read me.

You.

So thank you, very much.

And Happy Thanksgiving.

ME, I WANT
A HULA HOOP

Daughter Francesca and I have been humming holiday music non-stop, which got us wondering why it's so appealing. I thought I'd let her answer that hard question, since I take only the easy ones, so she weighs in below:

Growing up, we always played the same three Christmas CDs: Frank Sinatra, Tony Bennett, and Charlie Brown. And I bought that Mariah Carey one, so I could listen to "All I Want for Christmas Is You" on repeat every year through most of the nineties. But now that I'm freshly on my own (and more interested in gifts under twenty bucks), everywhere I turn there is another recording artist promoting a new album of yuletide tunes.

No wonder performers love cranking out these holiday CDs; they get a free pass. Even obscure, outdated, or talent-challenged artists can put out a seasonal album, and we'll go easy on them. It's Christmas, after all.

But some stars really test our generosity. For instance, someone named Lady Gaga teamed up with someone named Space Cowboy to record "Christmas Tree." I don't know who either of these people is, but somehow I thought their title would be a little more creative.

Or take George Michael. He was arrested for crack cocaine possession in a public bathroom — not to be confused with his 1998 arrest for lewd conduct in a public bathroom — but that didn't stop him from recording a new holiday track, "December Song (I Dreamed of Xmas)." I'm all for second (or third, or fourth) chances, but I think it's safe to assume that George is on Santa's naughty list. He might have asked for community service, but he's getting a lump of coal.

The all-time lows of Christmas music have to be those *Jingle Dogs* and *Cats* albums, where dogs bark and cats meow to the tune of holiday classics. Have you longed to hear "Angels We Have Heard On High" in a head-splitting caterwaul? Me neither.

It's a shame there aren't as many Hanuk-kah albums, but on the upside, at least they don't have cats singing, "Dreidel, dreidel, dreidel."

To me, Josh Groban is the newborn king of the modern holiday CD. His *Noël* was last year's biggest-selling album of any genre. That floppy-haired cutie with the powerhouse pipes gets me — and 3.7 million other people — every time.

So why do we buy these holiday albums? We often say holiday music puts us in the "holiday spirit," but what do we mean?

I read somewhere that music directly accesses the emotional part of the brain, and I believe it. Music is a language that our hearts and souls can speak. The holidays are a time when we want to get into an emotional and spiritual frame of mind, and these songs unlock something inside us. That Sinatra album is the same music that played when I was little, unwrapping presents in our apartment. The Charlie Brown CD my mom will put on this year is the same that was playing the year that our old dog Lucy, then just a puppy, knocked over the Christmas tree. The songs Josh Groban sings are the same that I sang when my high school chamber choir went caroling in the halls.

I love that music, because I love those memories.

These songs remind us of family, childhood, a time when it was safe to be vulnerable and safe to believe. After a year of steeling ourselves against life's hardships, now is a time when we can let down our guard. Music softens us, so that we can come into the warmth of family and un-bundle, so to speak. Because at some point, when everyone is gathered around the table, talking over each other and laughing, and the voices get louder, some voices you hear every day and some not often enough — well then, anything else is just background music.

PLAYING CHICKEN

I'm a fan of the hum-a-few-bars-and-I'll-play-it school. I mean, I like to throw myself into new things and I figure I'll learn along the way. It's worked so far, for everything in my life except romance and chicken farming.

Today, we discuss the latter.

You may remember the chickens I got, fourteen in all, a complete array of Gilbert & Sullivan hens and a Women's Chorus of Plymouth Barred Rocks. I've watched them grow from chick to full-grown, so now they're all chubby and feathery and friendly. They let me pick them up and turn them over on their backs, which is hypnosis for chickens, and they become calm, cradled in my arms and looking up at me, blinking their round amber eyes. I call this game Baby Chicken, which I'm sure has nothing to do with me being an empty nester.

I installed a baby monitor in the chicken

coop, which may sound a little strange, but why stop now? I'd never heard of a baby monitor in a chicken coop, but it turned out to be a fun idea. I keep it on all day long at the house, so I can work listening to the pleasant cooing, clucking, and occasional squabbling you would expect from a house that holds more than two females of anything, especially if they have beaks, nails, and major attitude.

It's a hen party, 24-7.

So far, so good until one of my other bright ideas, which is to let the chickens out every day so they can run around free. I started doing this in the summer, and they loved it, either foraging in the grass for delicious bugs or digging to China, for all I know.

It's a chicken thing.

I knew that they weren't safe from foxes or raccoons, so I stood guard and watched them bask in the sun, roll in the dirt, or cluster together to form some kind of chicken molecule. Don't ask me why they do this, either. I'm new here.

Then I noticed that they like to migrate together into the barn, and I let them because I figured they'd be safe from predators on the ground and from the sky, because they were under a roof. In time, I became a little more lax about standing guard, and they were outside all day, loving their very free-range life.

So you know where this is going.

Disaster struck.

I was in the backyard with daughter Francesca, the chickens were in the barn, and all of sudden, a hawk dive-bombed out of nowhere after them. Francesca and I started running, the hawk flew away, but we got there too late. A member of the Women's Chorus was dead on the floor and the other chickens were terrified, squawking and calling, scattering all directions.

We managed to get all of them back into the coop, except for one that was hiding under the straw, flattened in fear, and two others we discovered with the help of Ruby The No-Longer-Medicated Corgi. She found the chickens standing completely still under a bush, pretending to be lawn ornaments.

So I consulted my chicken books and ended up buying an electrified fence, which took all morning to install, but then I couldn't bring myself to shock my babies or turn my backyard into a Kentucky Fried Chicken. Then I realized what I really needed was overhead netting, so I got one online and spent all day trying to stretch it on top of the electrified fence, which turned out to be too flimsy to support even itself, and the whole thing collapsed into an expensive mess. So now I'm trying to figure out how to build some sort of outside cage that will keep them safe from hawks, raccoons, and my other mistakes.

Come to think about it, it's not so different from raising kids. All parents start out as rookies, and we learn as we go, making mistakes as we let our children explore. There will be trials and errors both, but parents learn from their mistakes, too, and if we're lucky, we'll all survive the hawks we meet along the way.

And even chicken parenting has its perfect moments.

Daughter Francesca and I took Mother Mary into the coop the other day, and were happily surprised to find that one of the Araucana chickens had laid her first egg — small, perfect, and blue as clear sky.

I'd count that as graduation day, wouldn't you?

LIFE DURING WARTIME

History is littered with famous battles, but even the biggest pale in comparison with the battles in the Scottoline house hold when my mother is in for a visit. We make the Punic Wars look puny.

Two of my favorites are the Battle of the Hearing Aid and the Battle of the Thirty-Year-Old Bra.

The first shot in the Battle of the Hearing Aid is fired as soon as my mother gets off the plane. Daughter Francesca and I meet her at terminal B and ask, "How was your flight?"

"Red," my mother answers, giving us a big hug.

"Did you get any sleep?"

"Seven thirty," she says, with a sweet smile. Francesca and I exchange glances, and we group-hug her to the car. She insists on sitting in the back seat, where she won't be able to see our faces, losing all visual cues of what we're saying, which guarantees that the conversation will be a string of non sequiturs until the shouting starts.

"Ma, did you get anything to eat on the plane?" I ask, raising my voice.

Total silence.

"Ma, did they feed you on the plane?"

More silence.

"MA, ARE YOU HUNGRY? OR CAN YOU WAIT UNTIL WE GET HOME?"

"What?"

"MA! YOU WANT TO EAT OUT OR GO HOME?!"

You see the problem. I'm exhausted from her visit and we haven't even left the car. Already my emotions are swinging from guilt to resentment, the drama pendulum. Mother Mary is a funny, smart, and talkative lady, but if she can't hear, she'll eventually check out of the conversation, and in time I'll get tired of repeating and shouting, so I'll talk as if she isn't there.

By the way, she already has a hearing aid, which took the Boer War for her to get, but she needs a second one. I cannot understand why the second hearing aid has become such a Donnybrook. If you have the first one, what's the big deal? You're no longer a hearing aid virgin.

Plus, I had asked her to get another hearing aid as my Christmas present, which gives me a powerful weapon for my battle plan. I ambush her at dinner, sneak-attacking. "Ma, I can't believe you didn't get the second hearing aid, for Christmas."

Her snowy head remains down, and she stabs a piece of salmon with her fork, which means either that she didn't hear me or she's formulating her counter-offensive. Don't underestimate her just because she's older. Experience molds great generals. Patton was no kid, and Mother Mary makes him look like Gandhi.

"MOM, WHY DIDN'T YOU GET THE SECOND HEADING AID?"

She looks up calmly and blinks her brown eyes, cloudy behind her bifocals. "Why are you shouting at me?"

"I DON'T KNOW. MAYBE BECAUSE YOU DON'T HAVE A SECOND HEARING AID? JUST A GUESS."

"How can you start in with that while I'm eating? You'll make me choke." Whereupon she flushes red and begins a coughing fit that ends with her clutching her chest.

Ka-boom! My barrage of guilt infliction is blown out of the water by a fake cardiac arrest.

I never had a chance.

The Battle of the Thirty-Year-Old Bra

begins when she puts on the stretchy shirt we gave her for Christmas and declares that it doesn't fit correctly. You don't need to be on Project Runway to see the problem. The shirt doesn't have darts at the waist, and her breasts are in Australia.

"Ma, the shirt is fine. You need a new bra."

"What?"

"HOW OLD IS YOUR BRA?"

"Since when is that your business?"

"YOUR BREASTS ARE TOO LOW!"

"Look who's talking."

She has a point. I'm not wearing a bra, but I hear they work miracles if you actually care. I'm braless unless I have a book signing. Then I haul out my underwire, which is heavy artillery for girls.

Francesca says, gently, "If your bra is older than two years, the elastic has given out. Is it older than two years?"

Are you kidding? I think, but keep my own counsel. I haven't bought a bra in five years and I know Mother Mary hasn't bought one in ten. I would guess that her bra is twenty years old or maybe even thirty. In fact, I'd bet money that her bra's in menopause and a member of AARP.

I could continue the story, but you get the idea. She admits that her bra is thirty years old, but she won't get a new one, which doesn't matter as much as a hearing aid, and though I pick my battles, in the end, I lose them all.

It's no coincidence that Mother Mary and Napoleon Bonaparte are about the same height.

CRYBABY

For someone who has almost no estrogen, I sure do cry a lot. I don't mean in a bad way, but in a good way. I find myself moved to tears a lot lately, and by lately, I mean the past thirty years.

I used to cry whenever daughter Francesca was onstage, anywhere, doing anything. You should have seen me at her college graduation. I was positively deranged. The people sitting around me recoiled, and in the pictures from that day, I look drunk.

This past holiday season, I cried almost all the way through the Charlie Brown Christmas special. The waterworks began as soon as those cartoon kids started singing. When their mouths formed those perfect little circles, I simply could not deal.

I cry at all kinds of movies. I watched *Fred Claus* on TV and cried like a baby. Who cries at a Vince Vaughn movie? Worse, in a Gift-of-the-Magi moment this past Christmas, I gave Francesca a copy of Stephen Colbert's holiday DVD, and she gave me one, too. When we watched it later, I cried at the end, when Stephen sings about believing in God.

It's a *comedy* videotape.

I cried when I got my new puppy, too. The breeder, a lovely woman named Tina, put him in my arms, and I exploded with estrogen. Now I know why I have none left. It leaks out of my eyes whenever it gets the chance.

The latest example of what a crybaby I am took place when I took Mother Mary to the airport to go back to Miami. I know you're thinking that I was crying because she was leaving, but to be completely honest with you, I'm not sure that's the case. She'd been visiting me for a long time, and even the most devoted daughter will tell you that it's never a hundred percent bad to put your mother on a plane outta town.

And most mothers would admit that, too.

So imagine my surprise when I started to get teary before we'd even reached the airport. I was so misty I couldn't even find a parking space. If you're weeping in short-term parking, do you have a problem?

Am I an estrogen junkie? A woman? Or merely Italian-American?

I managed to keep it together when we checked her in at the ticket counter and I asked for a pass to walk her to the gate. I do this because she sometimes gets confused, and you know how she feels about wheelchairs.

The same as she feels about second hearing aids.

So we had a bite to eat and I walked her to the plane, but by the time I hit the jetway, the tears were flowing like cheap wine. Mother Mary ended up comforting me.

"I'll be alright, honey," she said. "Hey, maybe I'll meet somebody on the plane. You never know."

Which only made me cry harder. Besides the fact that she had to cheer me up, I've had the same pathetic fantasy myself, and it's never true. The only men you meet on the plane are married, which is the second worst thing about airplane travel, after honey pretzels.

Anyway, by the time we were at the door of the plane, I was such a basket case that the flight attendant rushed toward me with a cocktail napkin, for me to wipe my eyes. I swear to you, this is God's truth. Her name was Susan, and she was on flight number 1651, USAir from Philly. Susan held me close while we discussed how much we loved our parents and she told me that she used to cry when she put her father on a plane, too.

By the way, Mother Mary was fine.

She found her way to her row by herself, and another flight attendant hoisted her roller bag into the overhead. She plopped herself into her seat, clutching her wrinkled plastic bag of crossword puzzle books, her special red pens, and a magnifying glass for when she reads. I got her a better one for Christmas, a big round circle, and when she uses it, she looks like a superannuated Nancy Drew.

I gave her a sloppy kiss on the cheek, then sobbed my way off the plane and back through all the people in the airport, who averted their eyes. I've learned that's what most people do when you make a complete fool of yourself in public.

But there's always a few of them who look back.

They're the ones who can't watch Charlie Brown, either.

BESTIES

Many of us pet fanatics will admit that we learn life lessons from our dogs and cats, but few will go so far as to say that their role model is a puppy.

I will.

Let me tell you the story of Little Tony, my insanely plucky black-and-tan King Charles Cavalier puppy.

If you think you've got problems, Little Tony's started on his second day of life on the planet, when his mother accidentally chewed off his foreskin, along with his umbilical cord.

Thanks, Mom.

I'm told he didn't even whimper in protest, and this I believe. Nothing gets this puppy down, even though he's more anatomically incorrect than a Ken doll. And every time he pees, it looks like a sprinkler went off.

All over his four legs.

Now, I ask you, if every time you went to the bathroom, you had to change your pants, wouldn't you whine? No? Now how about if you had to change your sweater, too, and then wash the floor? In short, what if, most of the time, you could pass for a rest stop on the turnpike?

Not to mention that he's missing most of what is some men's favorite organ. And it was his own mother who emasculated him. It gives new meaning to the term castrating bitch.

This would cause psychological problems of major proportions in mostly anybody, or at least entitle them to a guest shot on Dr. Phil.

But Little Tony's fine with it.

This is a dog who could be sending Medea a greeting card on Mother's Day, yet he never whines about Mom or anything else.

In short, in all things, he's relentlessly Cavalier.

This may sound tautological, but he's happy because he's happy. It's simply an act of will, on his part. It's not a matter of not sweating the small stuff; it's not sweating anything at all. Ever. Now and forever. He's just a rolling ball of good will, positive energy, and fun.

And as a result, miracles happen.

I say this because, if you recall, my dog family includes Penny and Angie, mellow golden retrievers, which is redundant, and the control freak of the canine world, Ruby The Corgi. Ruby's not a bad dog, she's just territorial, and her territory is the Northern Hemisphere.

If you live here, it's only because she forbears.

Maybe because she's a herding dog, Ruby feels the need to order the comings and goings in everyone's daily life, and that includes mechanical objects. She barks if cell phones ring without permission. Computer printers produce major affronts. Vacuum cleaners declare war.

Because she has so much responsibility, it's tough to be Ruby. She was on Prozac for a while, but that didn't work. Maybe next we'll try Pilates.

The problem is, she's the world police, so she can never rest. She watches everything. She's alert to every sound. She keeps dogs, cats, and chickens in line. She's the one who tried to bite my old golden retriever Lucy, and I got caught in the crossfire, sending me to the ER without a bra.

But that's another story.

Bottom line, Ruby doesn't play well with others. When daughter Francesca's new puppy Pip entered her universe, Ruby morphed into the ultimate Mean Girl. So I knew that if I got a new puppy, I was in for dog management problems, if not the battle of the century.

But what do you think happened?

What results when endless good meets endless, well, Ruby?

I warn you, my specialty is the surprise ending.

Ruby loves Little Tony.

Wonder of wonder, miracle of miracles.

From the first moment Little Tony set his tiny black paw in this house, Ruby adored him. They play together all day. They sleep together at night. They share Nylabones and tennis balls. They even share food.

They are BFFs.

I cannot explain this remarkable turn of events. It's so sappy, it doesn't even happen in greeting cards.

All I can do is learn from it.

Little Tony is my new guru.

And I'm never complaining about Mother Mary, ever again.

News Flash

I woke up this morning with the best hot flash I ever had. This was such a good hot flash that if I smoked, I would've reached for a cigarette.

If you get my drift.

Oh. My. God.

Blood seemed to rush all over my body, from everywhere at once, to everywhere at once, setting every inch of me tingling. My puppy Little Tony, who had been sleeping in the crook of my arm, looked up at me in amazement.

I asked him, "Don't you wish you were a middle-aged woman?"

So let me say a word or two about hot flashes, because the fact is, I'm a big fan.

To back up a minute, it's amazing that I have yet to discuss hot flashes, because usually, they're my second or third conversational subject, after hair products and carbohydrates.

I know I'm not alone in this, at least among women. Cross the threshold of any ladies' room, and all anybody is talking about is their hair, their kids, their weight, and their hot flashes.

Don't go cranky on me.

I'm not being sexist or saying that women can't discuss politics, the economy, or the stock market, but that isn't the stuff we're talking about in the ladies' room. A ladies' room is a girl headquarters, where everybody reapplies eyeliner that doesn't need reapplying, squeezes back into pantyhose, and continues conversations into the stalls. Nobody cares enough about the stock market to take it into the stalls.

Kids, yes.

Hot flashes, definitely.

Most women I know complain about "flashing," as the doctors call it, and I used to, before I met Little Tony and began my really annoying crusade of positivity. So this is how I look at hot flashes now:

They're a godsend.

Observe.

I don't know about you, but I was cold for approximately the first forty years of my life. In winter, I'd freeze my butt off, and in summer, I hated air-conditioning. I used to fight with everybody over the thermostat, and I never won. I was always the coldest person in the room, and so were all my women friends.

No longer.

Hot flashes are God's way of compensating women for all the years they spent being cold.

Now, we will be toasty no matter what the weather, and all we have to do is get old. It doesn't even take any effort or cost anything. All we have to do is keep breathing, and all of us, our gender entire, will be wrapped up in a permanent burrito of thermal pleasure.

It's like we'll all have our own Snuggie fleece blanket, as Seen On TV, only we don't have to walk around looking like monks.

And don't forget the other advantage of flashing, namely the aforementioned tingling.

Let's talk turkey.

There are times in life when we have to settle for second best. For example, we would love to have a hamburger, but we settle for the veggie burger. Or we would love to have a gorgeous Chanel purse, but we settle for the look-alike.

So you know where this is going.

Think of a hot flash that way, if you follow.

If it makes you tingle all over, sets your blood pounding, raises your body temperature, and usually happens in bed, wouldn't you settle for a hot flash?

If it walks like a duck and talks like a duck, why split hairs?

Plus, you can be alone and get a hot flash. You don't have to marry and divorce anyone. Or worse, share your closet space.

I think it's all part of God's divine plan, sending us hot flashes at a time in our lives when the real deal tends to be in shorter supply. Everybody's sex life diminishes as they get older, and kids and carbohydrates don't help.

Neither does the stock market.

So I say, look forward to your next hot flash. If you're lucky, you can have five or six a night.

There's nothing wrong with multiples.

PAY TV

I read that most adults spend three to five hours a day watching TV, but I don't believe it. Know why?

The only shows on TV are Paid Programming. The other day I was trying to find something to watch, and everywhere I looked, it was all Paid Programming, one hour after the next.

What gives? When did this start? And, more importantly, how can we kill it?

I never noticed these Paid Programming shows before. I thought only the commercials were paid programming, but no. I tuned in to one to see what it was, and it was a guy selling special brushes. On another, a guy sold special floor cleaners. On a third, a guy sold special weight-loss herbs. I remained unsold. If they're so special, why aren't they on Unpaid Programming?

Plus, the programming was so bad, they should pay us to watch it. Then they could call it Pay Us Programming.

Not to mention the fact that we pay for all these extra cable channels to show us the Paid Programming. Uh, I think I just figured out why they call it that — because somebody paid the cable company to show it. In that case, since the cable company got paid by the advertiser and by us, they should change the name. To Sucker Programming.

Who watches Paid Programming, anyway? It's a mystery. Are there really people in the world who would sit down and watch an hour-long commercial? If there are, they should show themselves, and we should all gather around them and be their friend, in shifts.

Of course, there are no commercial interruptions in Paid Programming, because it's all commercial. It makes for a weird viewing experience. I think they should interrupt Paid Programming every ten minutes with seven minutes of a sitcom like *Friends* or *Seinfeld.* Then we could fast-forward through the sitcom to get to the commercial.

Fun!

But the mystery of Paid Programming pales in comparison with the other shows on the TV listings. I was skimming the guide and came across something on Channel 28 called Educational Programming (EDUC). I tuned in, but the screen was blank. I kept waiting for someone to educate me, or failing that, a guy to sell me something special, but no, nothing.

This doesn't bode well for our educational system.

It's like No TV Left Behind.

I kept spinning the dial, as we used to say, and came upon an equally ambiguous listing on Channel 98, called Local Original Programming (LO). I tuned in, and it was showing a man and a woman talking to each other, neither of whom seemed very interested in the conversation.

In other words, my second marriage.

I would rename Channel 98 The Strike Two Channel (LOSER). Or maybe The What-Were-You-Thinking? Channel (GET OUT WHILE YOU CAN).

Either way, you couldn't pay me enough to watch that programming.

I kept looking for something else to watch, as I had three hours of mandatory viewing left to fill, and I came across Channel 22, which purported to be Government Access Programming (GA).

Wrong.

It had nothing to do with government, but

was Paid Programming In Disguise, namely, a series of real estate ads. ("Rear Fenced Yard!" "Six Years Young!" "Family-Friendly Spaces!"). Likewise, The Information Channel (INFO) had nothing to do with information, but was more Paid Programming In Disguise, albeit for non-profit organizations. ("Monthly Sunday Breakfast!" "Annual Spaghetti Dinner!" "Winter Dance!") I watched for ten minutes and came to the realization that Paid Programming for non-profits is just like Paid Programming for profits, except with worse music.

Things picked up when I got to Channel 166, The Fear Channel (FEAR). It was showing something called FearNet On Demand, so I clicked and got a menu of scary choices such as Blood & Guts, From Beyond, and Interrogation Room. I looked for The Economy, but they didn't have it.

That's probably on The Apocalypse Channel (PUT ALL YOUR MONEY IN A MATTRESS).

Or The Armageddon Channel (NOW GRAB THAT MATTRESS AND RUN FOR THE HILLS).

Or The End-Of-Life-As-We-Know-It Channel (AND REMEMBER, THE BEST THINGS IN LIFE ARE FREE).

Anyway I was too scared to click on any

of the Fear categories, but I applaud the idea of a Fear Channel. Why shouldn't there be channels devoted to the major emotions? I'd like to see a Love Channel (CHOCOLATE CAKE). And a Hate Channel (LIVER WITH ONIONS).

And a Lust Channel. (GEORGE CLOONEY).

(WITH CHOCOLATE CAKE).

CREAMY

I never use any moisturizer on my face at night, but when I went to visit daughter Francesca in New York, she and her roommate smeared cream all over their faces before they went to bed.

And their combined age is still less than mine.

So I thought, I should do this. I should take a lesson from the kids. Maybe if I used a moisturizer at night, my face wouldn't look like a roadmap of wrinkles, with I-95 running parallel to the turnpike on my forehead. So I went home, dug some cream out of the closet, spackled my cheeks, and went to bed. Which is just when Little Tony the puppy trotted over to my pillow and sat on my face.

Whoever said you should use a night cream didn't have a dog who sleeps on their cheek.

To interrupt the story, I never had a dog

sleep anywhere near my head, much less on my face. All my dogs always sleep at the foot of the bed, and it works out just fine. My feet are always warm, and I doze off listening to the rhythm of their contented snoring.

It's like Ambien, only with fur.

But Little Tony, the new black-and-tan Cavalier puppy, sleeps on my pillow, with his head resting on my cheek or my neck. I know it sounds weird, but it's cute, cozy, and fun. I highly recommend it, if your social life is at an all-time low, too.

In any event, I forgot about this habit of Little Tony's as I put on the night cream, so when he plopped his puppy tushie on my cheek, it took me a second or two to understand the implications. And by the time I detached his butt from my face, stray black hairs clung to my cheek like a beard.

Not a good look, for a single gal.

Of course, I didn't give up, as I need both smooth skin and warm puppy, so since then I've gone to bed with the night cream and Little Tony, craning my neck to keep his fur off my face, or my face off his fur, generally twisting and turning most of the night until we both fall into an exhausted, albeit glossy, sleep.

The plot thickens when Little Tony has

the first of what would be three operations. As you may remember, the poor little guy had a mother who accidentally bit off his foreskin, evidently taking literally the term "castrating bitch."

In any event, he needed an operation to reconstruct his foreskin, but it came out too big. So he had a second operation, but it came out too small. He just had his third operation, and this time it's just right.

It's like Goldilocks, only with, well, you get it.

Why this matters is that after each of these operations, he had to wear one of those plastic Elizabethan collars for dogs, shaped like a cone over his head. He wears it for two weeks after every operation, and with three operations, he has spent six weeks of his young life in the plastic collar, or, as I call it, the Tony Coney.

So you know where this is going.

If you thought it was crazy to have dog face stuck to your night cream when you sleep, try wrapping that puppy in a plastic cone, slapping it on top of your face cream, and trying to catch forty winks.

It's fun.

The only experience I've had like this happened ages ago, when I was in sixth grade, trying to clear up a case of adolescent acne by using Cuticura ointment. Please tell me I'm not the only person in the world who remembers old-school Cuticura. I went online before I wrote this and am astounded that the product still exists, though I'm sure it's improved.

It would have to be.

Back then, it was a round orange tin full of smelly, gooey, black-green gunk. Somebody told my mother it was good for pimples, but they must have been criminally insane. In retrospect, it was good for greasing axles. Yet I smeared it faithfully on my skin every night, reeking like a motor pool, and every morning my skin looked worse.

In any event, I digress. My fancy night cream is better than Cuticura, even though I get the occasional dog-hair sideburn. Two weeks later, I am sleepless but happy, but there's not a wrinkle on Little Tony.

So maybe it works.

THE VALUE
OF MONEY

Now that we have an economic stimulus plan, everybody is trying to figure out how it will work.

Me, I opt out.

I'm trying to figure out how Jennifer Aniston spent $50,000 on her hair during her movie tour to London and Paris.

I'm not sure she got her money's worth, unless they blew her dry with gold.

Although I admit, there's part of me that gets it. Hair matters to women. If I won the lottery, I might pay somebody $50,000 for great hair. In fact, I bet if you asked the average woman how much she would spend to get hair like Jennifer Aniston's, that woman would answer, "Anything."

So already, it's cheaper.

Plus, it's a bargain if you break it down by strand. By my calculations, Jen spent only fifty cents a hair. I got that number by going online and plugging "how many hairs on a woman's head" into Google. I didn't bother to verify the information. This is the comic relief department, remember?

Anyway, the computer reports that the number of hairs on a woman's head varies with her haircolor. Who knew? A blonde has 140,000 hairs on her head, but Jennifer Aniston isn't a natural blonde, because they're extinct. They died off millions of years ago in a meteor shower, or maybe they ran out of vegetation, scientists aren't sure, but either way, nowadays we all highlight our hair and forget our natural color.

People with brown or black hair have 110,000 strands, but the computer says that the average person has 100,000 hairs. I used 100,000 because it's easier and I hate math.

Therefore, Jen spent fifty cents a hair.

That's nothing. I can't remember the last thing I bought for fifty cents. Chewing gum costs twenty-five dollars, and sandwiches are a million. Your basic bailout starts at ten billion, and we owe China twenty trillion, so why split hairs?

Sorry.

By the way, the same week that Jen spent $50,000 on her hair, Patriots Quarterback Tom Brady bought a Rolls-Royce Phantom for $405,000.

He also got married to Gisele Bündchen,

and I sense that these things are not unrelated. If you're gonna marry Gisele Bündchen, you're not carting her around in a Ford Fiesta.

She's tall.

The news also reported that Tom Brady put a baby seat in the Rolls-Royce, for the child he conceived with the woman whose name he forgot when he met Gisele Bündchen.

But that's not my point.

I'm trying to understand how Tom could spend $405,000 on a car. To be fair, men do love cars. I bet if you asked the average man how much he would pay to drive Gisele Bündchen around in a car, that man would answer, "Anything."

So $405,000 is a bargain.

I went online to the Roll-Royce website and learned that the Phantom has four "coach" doors, which means that the back doors are hinged wrong and open in a counterintuitive way. But they're only $100,000 a door, so it's still cheap.

Also the Phantom has a statuette on the hood, which looks like a Barbie doll with wings. The statuette has a name, "The Spirit of Ecstasy," and if you take into consideration that you're getting the car, the Barbie doll, and the pornographic name, then

$405,000 is more than fair.

Plus the Phantom has a quiet, powerful engine, specifically, "453 bhp at 5359rpm and 531 lb/ft 720 Nm at 3500rpm." I have no idea what that means, but I bet it translates to five miles a gallon.

So you see where this is going.

Buying a car for $405,000 is as crazy as spending $50,000 on hair, and it brings me to my point:

Cars are hair for men.

Conversely, hair is cars for women.

I doubt that a man would spend $50,000 on his hair, and no women I know would spend $405,000 on a car.

Now, here's the hard question:

Do men care if women have great hair?

No. If I were a woman who wanted to interest a man, I would take the $50,000 and buy the best breasts ever.

And do women care if men have great cars?

No. If I were a man who wanted to interest a woman, I would save the money and mow the grass.

And what have we learned?

The best things in life are free.

Or plastic.

UNDERGRADUATE

Little Tony and I just completed our first day of puppy kindergarten, and we flunked.

Of eight puppies, he was the worst in the class.

Where did I go wrong?

We were supposed to learn to Sit, but all Little Tony would do was Jump Up. We were supposed to learn Watch Me, but all he did was Watch Everybody Else. When it came to Take It, as in, wait until the command to eat his treat, he skipped the waiting part and went straight to That Tasted Great, Gimme More.

I should have known it would go bad from the beginning, at playtime. How can you flunk playtime? All puppies do is play, chew, and fart.

And he's very good at two of those things.

But at playtime, while all the puppies chased each other in a circle, nosed tennis balls around, or tugged pull toys, Little Tony sat shaking under my chair, his brown eyes round as marbles. If he was learning Look Terrified, he would have gotten an A plus.

The teacher tells me this will get better, but I'm hard pressed to understand a dog who acts terrified in public and, at home, morphs into Little Tony Soprano.

Oh wait.

Maybe that's human, after all.

It got me thinking that it would be useful if we could send people to puppy kindergarten. How great would it be to have your toddler Sit and Stay For Just Five Minutes?

And everybody wants a husband who can Watch Me. Too many husbands are only good at Watch Basketball. And too many wives are only good at Watch Out.

All most people want is a little attention. If we could just get people to Watch Me, then all manner of acting out could be eliminated. Lindsay Lohan would vanish from the tabloids. Paula Abdul would spontaneously combust.

I'd love to expand the curriculum, too. I wouldn't mind a guy who obeyed Listen To Me. Or better yet, Tell Me I'm Thin. And I'm sure that men can think of a number of commands they'd like women to obey, but I'm guessing that they're unprintable.

Also the teacher at the obedience school

told us that it follows the principles of Nothing in Life is Free. They mean this literally. Nothing-in-life-is-free even has its own website, NILIF.com, and ironically you can go visit it, for free.

I grew up hearing that nothing in life is free, but that turned out not to be true. Plenty in life is free. Going for a walk is free. Hugging is free. Money is free, if you're AIG.

Anyway, the bottom line of nothing-in-life-is-free for dogs is that you have to figure out what your puppy loves, and every time before you give it to him, you have to make him do something you want, like sit, stay, or please God stop having accidents all over the rug.

It seems kind of hardcore, for a puppy whose black-and-tan coat makes him look like a Reese's Peanut Butter Cup with legs.

So I tried nothing-in-life-is-free on Little Tony, because we're supposed to practice. One of Little Tony's favorite things, after anything edible, is sitting on my lap on the couch. Every night after dinner, the puppy will actually run to the couch, plop his tush on the floor, and wag his tail like a windshield wiper.

Adorable.

Except that I work a lot, so if I'm sitting,

I'm writing a book on a laptop, with the TV on. Now I have a puppy who's a laptop, but it's fun to type over a puppy head and my lap is warm at all times. Okay, maybe the space bar gets hit a thousand extra times, and my chase scenes are way too mellow, but it's a small price to pay.

I may switch to greeting cards.

Anyway, I tried to get Tony to obey Watch Me so we could sit on the couch, but no luck. He watched the other dogs, the cats, and even *Dancing With The Stars.* I tried for half an hour, then gave up. Meantime, he collapsed into an exhausted sleep, spreading out like melted chocolate, and I got no work done. My lap stayed cold, and I even missed *Castle,* a TV show about the exciting life of a bestselling writer.

Castle doesn't have a dog.

Poor thing.

MOM, INTERRUPTED

So I'm in New York, visiting daughter
Francesca for the weekend, which is just
the thing to remind you that your child is
more adult than you.

She drinks stronger coffee, wears high
heels with style, and could put on liquid
eyeliner, blind. Me, I'd blind myself with
liquid eyeliner.

We tool around the bustling streets, talking and walking with our two puppies in
tow, Pip and Little Tony. We pick up after
them, which is a change for me, because at
home I let them go in the backyard and call
it compost.

Little Tony, unaccustomed to life in the
big city, alternates between barking and
cowering. His threat detector is topsy-turvy,
so he growls at passing mastiffs while
pigeons send him scurrying in terror to my
feet. I try to not to reward fearful behavior,
but it's nice to still have something left

to protect.

My daughter is on her own.

And it's a good thing, but surprising.

All the things I used to do for her over the years, she now does for herself. I know it sounds obvious but it's still miraculous to me, if only because I can remember her first step. Now she does her own laundry, cooking, vacuuming, clothes to the dry cleaner, hanging up pictures, bed-making, getting prescriptions filled, and all of it, in the toughest, and most glorious, city on the planet.

New York doesn't intimidate her, even though the first week she was there, she witnessed a violent mugging on her street, a purse-snatching during which the woman's jaw was broken. A TV news crew arrived on the scene and interviewed Francesca, and she sent me the videotape from the station's website. Great.

Welcome to New York.

And it's time to let go. Again.

I've written before about how parenting is watching your child take a series of baby steps, all of them away from you, which is as it should be. It's both the happiest and saddest moments in the life of any mother and father. And it only gets harder, by which I mean, if you think letting them go to college was hard, try letting them move to New York, where it's not always easy for the puppies to tell the pigeons from the mastiffs.

Last night before bed, Francesca showed me a video game she plays on her BlackBerry, in which you make as many words as you can in thirty seconds, and as you get better, you advance through different seasons while the screen changes from winter to summer and back again. I normally hate video games, but I couldn't resist cuddling up with my big little girl, watching the seasons change in our hands.

My high score was 45. Hers was 4350.

For once, I'm not exaggerating.

I think we moms and dads play a sort of parental video game, where we complete one year to advance to the next, and all the time the years get harder and the little video rewards of fake-gold treasure chests or kelly-green shamrocks flash on the screen only to evaporate instantly, too fast to see. And so we tend to appreciate them in retrospect only, when the game is over and we play I Remember.

I remember your first word. Your first step. Your college graduation.

I remember because when we were making the memories, we were too busy to see, much less savor, the moment.

That's how we know we were good parents. Because we were too busy doing the laundry, cooking, vacuuming, clothes to the dry cleaner, hanging up pictures, bed-making, getting prescriptions filled, and, well, you get the idea.

People ask me where I get the ideas for my columns and books, and the answer is that they all come from my heart. I even wrote an entire book, *Look Again,* about the letting go of a child. In the book, a mother gets a missing child flyer in the mail, and the photo looks exactly like her adopted son. She has to answer the question — does her son really belong to another family, and if he does, should she keep him or give him up?

Oh, and by the way, she writes for a living.

I write what I know.

And what you know, too.

BABIES
HAVING BABIES

I am on tour for my new book, so I asked daughter Francesca to help me out, as she explains below:

When I was in high school, my mother's book tour meant that I had the house to myself, and I would spend the month eating a lot of spaghetti and Top Ramen noodles (cooking = boiling water), staying up late watching cable TV (swear words! edgy!), and cursing myself for not having the guts (or the contacts) to throw a totally sick house party. Instead, I was one of the kids who had her first sip of beer from my grandmother's Bud Light on Ice at ten years old and then not again until college.

I know. Lame.

Well, now I'm at the pinnacle of hip, young adulthood — I can order my *own* Bud Light on Ice, and I'm living in the Big City, the single mother to the cutest baby I know, my dog, Pip. I have a nice little routine — I work out at the local gym, I go to work, I walk the dog, I cook food that my roommate reluctantly but kindly eats, I get dressed up on the weekend in hopes of something exciting happening. Being a grown-up is easy!

But that's all about to change. I'm getting a new addition to my tiny family. And it was unplanned.

Little Tony is staying with me during my mother's book tour. He's the puppy my mother got just a few months after I got Pip. She and I are like the puppy version of Sarah and Bristol Palin; a mother-daughter team raising newborns at the same time. Listen, you can't plan these things, not around national book tours and not around presidential elections.

Every puppy is a blessing.

Just not *my* blessing.

See, there was a delicate balance to my life — one girl: one dog. This was enough to impress my friends, the way I blew right through the house-plant stage and onto the house-pet one (twenty-three-year-olds are easily impressed). But now, suddenly, there are two puppies in the house! Two dogs mean two walks, and two walks mean two pick-ups for two . . . well, you know. Who said I was ready for double duty? Much less double . . . ok, I'll stop.

And Little Tony is not city-savvy. Despite his wise-guy moniker, he's a backwoods doggie, through and through. Far from the rolling hills of Pennsylvania, he thinks peeing on the sidewalk is gross but peeing in the apartment is fun. When I walk him here, he growls at the passing Maltipoos and Labradoodles and Cockadoodle-dos, as if to curse them for their bedazzled collars and fancy grooming appointments. 'Go choke on your organic, free-range bison biscuit,' he seems to say! Pip tongues a piece of said biscuit still stuck in his teeth and feels embarrassed for everyone involved.

Me too, Pip, me too.

But when my mother called me a week ago, sounding stressed and worried about leaving her baby (Tony, not me) behind, I had to offer to take him, and truthfully, I wanted to. I'm happy to be able to actually help my mother with something.

I'm starting to realize that growing up is more than simply distancing myself from my parents. Learning to function as an independent entity, a family unit of one (plus a pet and some friends) is certainly part of it, but a joy and obligation of adulthood is learning to re-approach our parents, not as children, but as equals. All my life, my mother has loved and supported me, and growing up means returning the favor.

I'm lucky that my mother is healthy and young, and she won't need me to really take care of her for a good long time, if ever. But it's nice to know that on the rare occasions she does need a little help, I can say, "I'm here for you."

For all the car rides to play practice, hair blow-outs before the big dance, countless home-cooked meals, fashion second-opinions, career advising, sick-day chicken soup and movie marathons, post-breakup pep-talks, and phone calls for no reason but I'm walking somewhere and I'd like to hear her voice — to repay my mom for all that a mother does, let's just say, I would have to walk a lot of dogs.

ODE TO HALLMARK

Mother's Day is a good time to address the question of Hallmark holidays.

Bottom line, I'm in favor.

As in, two thumbs way up!

By way of background, a Hallmark holiday is defined by wikipedia.com, my guide in all matters, as "a disparaging term, used to describe a holiday that is perceived to exist primarily for commercial purposes."

In other words, Bah, humbug!

To which I say, Lighten up!

Why celebrate only for excellent reasons? Who can't be bothered to give a greeting card unless it's absolutely warranted? Or bring a present unless it's supremely well-deserved?

I celebrate any and all holidays, commercial or legit, religious or secular, without exception. Life is too short not to celebrate something, plus if you observe all the Hallmark holidays plus the national holidays, we're only talking about thirty days max, which is still just a third of the time Europeans take for vacation.

So kick up your heels!

Especially on Mother's Day.

Anyone who calls Mother's Day a Hallmark holiday has never given birth.

OMG.

How graphic do we need to get? If you were describing childbirth to an alien, where would you start? With the breathing and the sweating? With the contractions like Gas From Hell? With the fact that sometimes, as in my case, they had to fetch forceps and vacuums and everything else in the tool shed to yank daughter Francesca screaming from my body?

You're right. I don't deserve a greeting card.

I deserve a medal.

And a new car. Plus the Prize Patrol should pull up in front of my house with helium balloons and a giant check.

All moms deserve the same, whether they've been through childbirth or not, because we were there for our little monsters, whether they realize it or not. And before you get all feisty that I'm not including fathers, your day will come. But for now:

Happy Mother's Day!

Mothers are the ones on the front lines when noses leak, tears need to be wiped, and prom dresses selected. Moms did things for us we don't even realize and could never remember. We got to school each day, from kindergarten through middle school, washed and fed, lunches packed, with barrettes in our hair. How did that happen?

Moms.

I can't even begin to tell you all the great things Mother Mary did for me, starting with letting me make jokes about her herein.

When I was first published, she had a poster made that read LOCAL AUTHOR and drove around with it in the back window of her Dodge Omni. When I called to tell her that I made the *New York Times* bestseller list, she asked in amazement, "Does this mean that they read you in New York?"

"Yes," I replied.

She even called me last week after she heard about the swine flu, and told me not to eat bacon.

That's love.

It's not good information, but it's love.

In fact, basically any product recall, from peanut butter to baby strollers, she calls me. If a storm is heading my way, she calls me sooner than it's on TV. Doppler radar has nothing on Mary Scottoline.

Bottom line, she's thinking of me every minute, and any news she hears, she relates to me.

Anything I am I owe to Mother Mary.

Doesn't that merit a holiday?

A three-dollar card?

Some flowers? Chocolates? A book or a sweater?

Is a thank-you so out of the question?

Not to me. I'm on it.

Happy Mother's Day, Mom.

I love you.

And thanks.

UNMENTIONABLE

You may have heard about the bra that stopped a bullet. It happened in Detroit, where a woman heard a break-in at her neighbor's house, went to the window, and a bad guy fired at her. The bullet shattered the glass, but was deflected by the underwire in her Miracle bra.

It's a Miracle, right?

The story got me thinking that my underwire isn't working hard enough. It would never save my life. It won't even stay in place. All it does is ride up, making a red line across my breasts, as if it's playing Connect the Nips.

For this I paid $35.

I've come to the conclusion that underwear is not worth paying a lot of money for. Ladies, if you want to economize, your undies are the place to do it. Sorry, undies manufacturers. And especially Spanx makers. You know how I feel about you.

You'll get yours.

Anyway, why spend on undies? First off, nobody sees it. And if you're lucky enough for somebody to see it, chances are they've seen it before. In fact, if you're married, they've seen it 3,437,464 times before. By now they've memorized your bra rotation, including the one special bra that's your trump card.

Oh, admit it, girls. You have one. We all do.

You don't have to be a fembot to have a sure-fire underwire.

Even nuns like me have a Good Bra. For church.

But the truth is, the trump card loses its effect over time. Men develop an immunity, especially if the ball game is on. I've never met the push-up that can face down a World Series.

Let's get real.

I never knew a lot about men to begin with, and I remember even less, but as I recall, they don't really care about bras. It's skin they're after. If you really want to please a man, I'd save on underwear and put the money into NFL Season Ticket on cable.

In fact, it makes me wonder whether men would spend what we do on undies. Take thongs, for example. I doubt you could talk a man into a thong, at any price. Men want cotton and comfort. They know their trump card is a steady job.

I went through that phase where people told me that thongs were "so comfortable." Liars, every last one of them. Thongs are comfortable only if you're a fan of shoelaces. I saw that movie *Man on Wire,* about a Frenchman who walked a tightrope between the towers of the World Trade Center. At one point, he sat on the tightrope and winced.

That's as close as a man will get to a thong.

Plus, the less comfortable the thong, the more it costs. I saw thong prices go from twenty bucks to thirty, and I went back to my Hanes three-pack of cotton bikinis. Why pay more, for panties? In the end, I know they're just going to end up as chew toys for the dog. My goldens stroll downstairs with them hanging between their teeth, usually when the UPS man is here.

Hi!

Plus cotton undies take no care at all. Throw them in the washer with your sweat socks and go. Even the Sturdy cycle, they can handle it. They're Sturdy, by God!

Contrast that with the care and feeding of

your thongs. Children need less attention. The woman at the store told me I had to wash my thongs by hand, in warm water and Woolite, then lay them flat to dry. I did that approximately one time. I washed my thongs and set them drying on towels arrayed on the kitchen table. Which was when the UPS man came in.

The curse of working at home is that the UPS man knows way too much about you. The upside is, you don't care.

So I went back to the store and they told me I could put the thongs in the washing machine, but I would need a special mesh laundry bag to protect them from the mean old hot water. And thongs have to be washed on the Delicate cycle, which I always forgot to put on. In time, they turned into expensive slingshots, and I gave up.

I'm Sturdy, not Delicate.

And I expect as much from my undies, even if they don't save my life.

Author Barbie

Before I left for book tour, I had to get my roots done and buy new jeans.

This would be the proverbial good news and bad news.

I love getting my roots done, because it makes me feel like a natural blonde for one whole day. I try to schedule as many things as I can that day, just so I can stay out and march around, tossing my head like a shampoo commercial. Later I drive home fast, with the sunroof open.

Wheee!

Blondes do have more fun.

But my blondeness evaporates by the next day, when I start to see a line of darkness advancing from my hairline like a storm cloud. In more recent years, I've begun to notice a few strands of gray — okay, maybe more than a few, like maybe Elsa Lanchester in *The Bride of Frankenstein.*

Not a good look for me.

To tell the truth, lately I'm longing for my black roots. In fact, I might even start dyeing my roots black.

Or I could just save the money and buy a Sharpie.

Either way, getting my roots done is fun, but shopping for jeans is my least favorite thing ever.

Please tell me I'm not alone.

Shopping for bathing suits gets all the bad press, but to me, shopping for jeans is much worse. If you're shopping for a bathing suit, you're steeled for bad news. Shopping for bathing suits is like the mammogram of clothes.

Plus, most people don't go bathing-suit shopping very often. I myself have been divorced as many times as I've gone bathing-suit shopping, not that there's any connection. My goal in life would be to get divorced more times than I've been bathing-suit shopping.

Then I could die happy.

But shopping for jeans can blindside you, and catch you unawares. It should be easy, but it's not. You might give yourself a day to find a pair of jeans, but that wouldn't be nearly enough. You have to factor in your shopping time, plus the times you give up and go home in disgust.

That's like twelve days, right there.

Buying jeans is much worse than buying swimsuits, mainly because there are five billion jeans companies and none of the sizes fit the same from one company to the next, except for one thing — the jeans are always too small.

Hmmm.

My favorite jeans used to be a super-comfy pair, but then people started telling me they were Mom Jeans. Evidently, I wasn't allowed to look like a Mom, though I was one, and everybody said that if I kept wearing the Mom Jeans, I'd live a Lifetime of Celibacy.

I'm halfway there.

So I went shopping for jeans, grabbed a bunch of pairs off the shelf, then went into the dressing room, trying on one after the other. Nothing fit right. I could barely get them closed in my alleged size, and if I went up in size, they gapped in the back. All of them were too long, like by a foot. Except for one magical pair. Amazingly, I slid into them and they fit perfectly, but they had a button fly.

Please.

The salesgirl came in, parted the curtain, and said, "Lots of women like button flies."

"They would be in AP Bio, right?"

She didn't reply and went away, so I tried on two more pairs with no luck, then slid into the third pair and struck gold. They fit great, closed easily, didn't gap at the back, and felt as good as my beloved Mom Jeans. The salesgirl came back, and I told her, "I love this pair!"

"Cool. They're so hot now. They're Boyfriend Jeans."

"What?"

"Boyfriend Jeans. You know, like if you stayed overnight at your boyfriend's and the next morning you put on his jeans?"

There were so many things wrong with what she was saying, I didn't know where to start. I reached out and closed the curtain in her face, then took off the jeans and left the mall, reeling.

So the only pants that fit me were men's.

And I didn't have a boyfriend.

And if I did, after I'd spent the night at his place, I would never dream of putting on his pants the next morning. That's why they call it cross-dressing.

Bottom line, I'm caught between Boyfriend Jeans and Mom Jeans.

I bet Hemingway didn't have this problem.

Meals on Wheels

I'm not sure when my car became my house, but I think it happened somewhere near Pittsburgh. And I bet I'm not the only woman who has a car house.

I've been driving around for book tour, so I've been on the road for about four weeks. And you know what? I love it.

I don't know if I'll ever move back home. My house is too big. And once you're inside it, you have to walk around. In other words, exercise.

In my car, everything I need is at my fingertips. I sit on my butt for miles and miles, yet I feel no shame. On the contrary, my car empowers me. The driver's seat is my cockpit, and I've become the Chesley "Sully" Sullenberger of my own life.

I can land my mothership anywhere. My parallel-parking skills have improved, and now I reverse with impunity.

Bottom line, I used to think of myself as a

homebody, but I've become a carbody.

I do everything in my car, like the classiest homeless person ever. I sing at the top of my lungs. I dance in the seat. I take naps, sleeping like a drunk with my mouth open. I know this because when I wake up, my lips are dry and droplets of drool encrust my chin.

I didn't say it was pretty.

I eat whenever I want, from drive-throughs. Or as we carbodies say, Drive Thrus. One banner day, I got my breakfast from a drive-thru Dunkin' Donuts (decaf with sesame bagel), lunch from a drive-thru McDonald's (Asian chicken salad without the chicken), and dinner from drive-thru Starbucks (turkey sandwich with iced green-tea latte). The day they build a drive-thru Sbarros, you'll never see me again.

I eat while I drive, even the salads. Here's my secret — don't dress it, forgo the fork, and use your hands.

Told you it wasn't pretty.

On the road I pass lots of other carbodies, all of us doing the same thing. Moms in packed minivans, sales reps with full closets in the back seat, lawyers writing on pads on the dashboard. They talk on phones or text like crazy. Once I saw someone smoking a cigarette, opening a pack of Trident, and driving at 70 mph. It was like watching someone juggle an axe, a gun, and a bazooka.

I always put makeup on in the car, since it has a great magnifying mirror, and I keep the mascara and blush in the glove box so it won't melt. Then I started moisturizing my legs in the car, and I pack the car moisturizer with two pairs of sunglasses, one prescription and one not, plus reading glasses, a spare pair of contact lens and big bottle of ReNu solution, so that my console is now my Eye & Beauty Centre.

I added my puppy, Little Tony, to the traveling circus, and he wowed the crowds at my signings and sold books like hotcakes. I pimped him out mercilessly. It's the least he can do, after I bought him a foreskin.

Those babies ain't cheap.

Little Tony has his own seat next to mine, and his own side of the car with his dog toys (plastic keys and Nylabones), bottle of water (Dasani) with paper cup (generic), snuggly blanket (adorable), and spare kibble (overpriced bullshiz). Still, it's nice to have a man around the house.

Last week, daughter Francesca and her puppy Pip came along for the ride, and soon my car house was bursting with mascara, kibble, and Snuggie blankets. Francesca rode around with two puppies on her lap, plus a chicken salad and drive-thru lemon cake. But in Arlington, Virginia, the air-conditioning broke down and the navigation system went on the fritz. The car house was melting down, and our road trip had come to an end.

On the way home, the car was quiet as we drove past the Washington Monument, all lit up, at twilight. It was a perfect white spire reaching heavenward, before a sky deepening to the hue of fresh blueberries and an orange moon proud as a newly minted penny.

"Check it," I said to Francesca.

But she was already looking.

Only the dogs missed it.

They were sleeping with their mouths open.

Heavy Cable

I give up. I admit it. I flunk multi-tasking.

Here's when I figured it out, finally:

I was in a hotel room watching MSNBC, as political pundits massaged an endless loop of the same election news. And at the bottom of the screen there were white banners with short phrases, evidently intended to explain the obvious, like OBAMA SPEAKING TO CROWD and MCCAIN LEAVING PLANE. Under the white banners was "the crawl," a moving line of script that reported the events of the day, from whoever hit the last home-run in Cincinnati to the stock market in Tokyo to new evidence that pomegranates aren't all they're cracked up to be. I tried to focus on the pundits but the crawl kept distracting me, and then five minutes later I was distracted even from the crawl by a bright red banner that came on and said BREAKING NEWS.

But BREAKING NEWS doesn't fool me

anymore.

I used to stop dead when BREAKING NEWS came on the screen, dropping my dishcloth in alarm. Now, I know better. Everybody who watches TV eventually figures out that BREAKING NEWS is neither breaking nor news. BREAKING NEWS is easily the most oversold phrase in the universe, after SUPPLY LIMITED and my personal favorite, LOSE FIVE POUNDS WITHOUT DIET OR EXERCISE!

To get back to my point, what happened was that I was trying to watch the pundits but I had to ignore the BREAKING NEWS banner, and the crawl was telling me something about a tornado in the Midwest, and I starting thinking about nice Midwestern people losing their homes and how they really deserved the BREAKING NEWS banner and not the crawl, which seemed like a demotion, and then I wondered if their insurance had been paid, which lead me to wondering if my insurance had been paid, and then what if there was a tornado that leveled my house and by the way, do I really want yellow shutters? I mean, who has yellow shutters?

BREAKING NEWS: CHOCOLATE CAKE IS DELICIOUS.

That was my chain of thought, and before you can say Benjamin Moore, one of the pundits had disenfranchised the voters of Florida, one of whom was my mother. Between us, I knew she wouldn't be happy about that. If my mother leaves the kitchen, she wants it to count.

BREAKING NEWS: IT'S GOOD TO HAVE FEET.

But the point is that I had lost track of what was going on because I was trying to ignore the BREAKING NEWS banners and trying to read the crawl, and then I tried to take in all three at the same time, which was impossible. Even if I managed to ignore the fake BREAKING NEWS, I got only the gist of the tornados and the gist of the primaries, and they both seemed like natural disasters.

I can't do two things at once, much less three.

I had the same problem last week, when I did my grocery shopping while I was on the cell phone. It seemed to be an efficient use of time, and I was continuing a conversation I had been having while I drove, which by the way, was hands-free. The only problem was that I went into the store for eggs, light cream, and romaine lettuce, and came out of the store, albeit hands-free, with the wrong kind of cream, a hunk of cheddar cheese, and spinach in a plastic box.

So I have to face the fact that I can't multi-task anymore. I used to be able to, but somewhere along the line, I lost my multitasking mojo. In a world of Black-Berries, cell phones, Sidekicks, and iPods, I don't know what to do about it.

I have to do more than one thing at once, or I won't get everything done. And I can't do away with my electronic toys, because I need them too much. For example, when Francesca was away at school, I loved sending her photos of the dogs from my Black-Berry, like the time Penny discovered the sunroof.

And daughter Francesca sends me cell phone photos when she's trying to decide which dress to buy, so I can see her wearing both. I don't think that's what shop-by-phone meant originally, but women are good at finding innovative ways to buy things.

We all know that our kids are texting, IM-ing, and calling each other all the time, bringing them closer to each other and making them happier, which is a good thing. And the devices can be lifesavers — calling for directions in a pinch or texting to find your kid, brother, and mother in a graduation crowd of 35,000.

So what's the answer?

BREAKING NEWS: THERE ARE NO ANSWERS.

PILLOW TALK

One of the great things about getting older is that you're tired enough to fall asleep, all the time. Or maybe it's that you realize you're not missing anything if you nod off. You know that it will all be there when you wake up, for good or ill. This might be called perspective.

Or laziness.

For example, I never used to be able to take a nap, but now I'm a big fan. I love naps. When I told a friend about this, she called them power naps. She said, "After you take one, you can work harder."

Not exactly.

To me, the term "power nap" is an oxymoron. I don't take power naps. I take out-of-power naps.

I don't nap to work harder. I nap because I'm tired and I need to lie down.

I used to have all manner of sleep quirks. I couldn't sleep at night unless the room was completely dark, absolutely quiet, or if there was a man next to me.

Then I got over it. My second divorce cured me.

Nowadays I have no curtains on my bedroom windows, and daylight streams in at dawn, but it doesn't wake me. Nothing wakes me, these days. Here is a true story — a few years ago, a fire broke out in a field next door to my house, and it took ten firetrucks all night to extinguish. I slept through it. Why?

I was tired.

But I relapsed on book tour, in different hotel rooms for four weeks, and I got to thinking that I couldn't sleep unless it was dark. Hotels have those double curtains; you know the ones, the top curtain made of some lovely fabric and behind it the secret curtain, made of gray impermeable rubber to block out light, noise, and nuclear war.

I closed the curtains, using that weird plastic wand, went to bed, and settled down. Then I noticed the flashing red lights on the fire detector and my BlackBerry. The phosphorescent glow of the digital clock. The red switch of a surge protector. The ghostly whiteness from the bathroom night-light. The hall light spilling under the door. The bright pinpoint of the laptop. The green of the thermostat.

Christmas in Room 373.

I got up and started unplugging things like crazy, turning over the BlackBerry, covering the thermostat with a towel, and tilting the alarm clock to the wall, but when I went back to bed, no dice. I reached for a pillow to burrow under, which was when I realized there were twenty-six of them on the bed. They were of all types and sizes; some were thick rolls like logs, and others were soft and square as ravioli.

I tried all the pillows, found some too hard and some too soft, then threw them off the bed like a latter-day Goldilocks, until I came to the widest and tallest pillow I'd ever seen, maybe six feet long and two feet wide. I turned on the light and called the front desk, "What's this big thing in my bed?"

"It's an organic body pillow."

Huh? For organic bodies? "What's that?"

"Our guests love our body pillows. They hug them. It's a sleep aid."

"Really? Thanks." I hung up, turned off the light, and flopped back down. After a minute, I leaned over and gave the body pillow an awkward hug. I admit it, I felt silly, looping an arm around an inanimate object. But it was kind of cuddly, and after a few minutes, it felt like a warm and friendly thing that I didn't have to marry and divorce.

I named him George.

As in Clooney.

Luckily I was in town for two dreamy nights, during which George and I slept happily together. I snoozed like a baby. So did he. It was hard to leave him, but we vowed there would be no strings. We made no promises we couldn't keep. When I had to move on, he didn't ask me to stay. In fact, he said nothing. He couldn't. He knew the way it was from the beginning.

I bet he's already sleeping with someone else.

With the curtains closed.

JITTERBUGGING

The Flying Scottolines are zooming around everywhere, like protons spinning crazily out of control. I may be wrong on the science, but I think this why we just had a familial nuclear explosion.

It started because I'm on book tour, brother Frank is visiting daughter Francesca in NYC, and Mother Mary is left at home in Miami.

Alone.

Without a cell phone.

In other words, she could fall and not get up. No one would know but two toy Pomeranians.

I find this unacceptable. I'm not her daughter for nothing. Mother Mary raised me to understand that the American home is a perilous place and lethal accidents can happen at any time. I'm still afraid my blow dryer will jump in the sink and electrocute me. Also I could choke if I eat too fast. Plus if you read without enough light, you could go blind.

I warned you. Don't come crying to me.

So you would think that she would understand my concern that she's home alone, with no cell phone in case of emergency.

But no.

Mother Mary resists getting a cell phone, on reflex. She fought a battle over the second hearing aid, and this is World War III. Her arguments are many: She doesn't need one. She won't fall. If she falls, she wouldn't want to get up right away, anyway. She could just lie there for a few days. It's cool on the floor. Bottom line, it's none of my business.

I rant, rave, and beg, but none of it works. I try scaring her. I tell her that if she didn't have a cell phone and she fell, she could die.

I actually said, "Ma, you will DIE!"

That's right, I threatened my own 84-year-old mother with the prospect of her own demise.

She said, "I'm not afraid of death. Death is afraid of me."

Finally I used my ultimate weapon. Guilt.

I told her, "You're worrying me, when I have to do my job on the road. I can't do my job because of you."

So now she has a cell phone. Or more accurately, a Jitterbug, which is like a cell phone for mothers. Of course, we fought over it for so long that brother Frank is now home, but never mind. She has it and that's good, though she doesn't agree. She describes it as "very pretty" but she has already decided not to use it, ever again. The buttons are big so she can see them, and she's supposed to wear it on a neck chain, but she won't. She admits it's easier than dialing the regular phone, but she hates it.

Let me tell you why.

Frank programmed it, then taught her how to answer and make a call. While he talked, she took notes in Gregg shorthand.

There is an irony to this, of course.

My mother was a secretary and always writes in shorthand, by habit. Most people don't even know what shorthand is, nowadays. I tell them it's like Swahili, without Africa.

Frank programmed five people on the Jitterbug's speed dial — himself, daughter Francesca, cousins Jimmy and Nana, and me. There's a big button for 911 and another for Operator, though I wonder how effective that can be. I tell my mother to forget the Operator button. I'm sure her call is important to them, but they will leave her to DIE.

Also let's not worry about the fact that the phone has a Philly area code and she lives in Miami. I don't want to think that the closest ambulance it calls is five days away.

Back to the story.

For their trial run, brother Frank told her to use the phone to call me and watched while she did it, with one gnarled finger placed purposefully on the button. But she seemed confused when the call connected. She said the phone wasn't working and tried to hand it back to Frank, but he insisted she use it. She kept trying to hand it back. It almost came to fisticuffs.

"Just talk into it!" he said.

"I don't know what to say," said she.

"Tell her we finally got the Jitterbug!"

So she did, telling about the new phone and its features. Then she hung up and handed the phone back to Frank, disgusted. "Throw this away."

"Why?"

"It didn't call Lisa. It called somebody else."

Frank checked the phone. He had pro-grammed my number in wrong, off by a digit. So Mother Mary had called a complete stranger and told her all about the new phone. He informed her as much.

"Told you," she said. "It sucks. It called some lady."

"So why did you talk to her?"

"You made me."

So for now, the phone remains in the wastebasket.

LIFE IN
THE MIDDLE AGES

I think I'm a woman "of a certain age," though when I tried to find a definition of the term, I couldn't. I checked online at dictionary.com, but it wasn't there, so I gave up.

Which is so like a woman of a certain age.

We have perspective.

In other words, I think I know the definition and I'm going with it. It isn't worth the time to look it up, especially when I could die at any minute.

Now, to begin.

I think a "woman of a certain age" means a woman in her fifties, though I've never heard the term applied to men in their fifties, which is odd. In any event, let's say that today I'm writing for men and women of a certain age.

We'll call it Life in the Middle Ages.

It's a weird time in lots of ways, but here's the way it's weird today. I'm thinking lately about Mother Mary, living in Miami with brother Frank. By way of background, until fifteen years ago, she lived in the house I grew up in, about five minutes from my house. She babysat for daughter Francesca while I worked part-time for the federal courts, before I was a writer. Then, after I finally got published (after five years of rejection, but that's another story), I stayed home, and my mother decided to move in with Frank.

We did talk about her living with me, but she thought my life was "too boring." She said, "all you do is read and write," which is true, except for the chicken part. Now, I feed chickens. I read, write, and feed chickens. I know it sounds boring, but it's my life's dream. And it's my blessing, or maybe my curse, to never be bored.

By anything.

Anyway, my mother lives down in Miami and she's happy as a clam. Brother Frank has tons of friends, all of whom are very attentive to mommies, and my mother goes out to dinner and has fun. I can barely get her to visit me for a long stretch because she misses her life, house, and dogs. So our time together is over the telephone, and if I don't call her for a few days, she'll say when she answers:

"Hi, stranger."

Or, "Who's this?"

Then we'll start talking about the weather or her eyes or who's sick in the family and stuff like that. Again, it's not boring, at least to me.

It's our only connection. I hear her voice, and she's hears mine. We laugh at things that only we think are funny, and every time we sign off, she says what she used to say before I went to bed — "pleasant dreams." I like the phrase so much that I stole it and say it to Francesca. Now, at the end of the phone call, my mother says it to me because she knows I like to hear it. Even at two o'clock in the afternoon.

And even though I'm a woman of a certain age.

But recently, I found myself thinking that, some day, my phone will ring, and it won't be Mother Mary. She has survived a world war and throat cancer, but one day, it will be Frank, calling me. And then he'll tell me what he has to say.

That will be how I find out.

As unimaginable as it is, I find myself imagining it more and more, with dread. Mostly these thoughts come to me at night, and then I can't sleep.

Pleasant dreams.

I don't know how to prepare for that phone call, and I wouldn't try even if I did. I'm just grateful for the time we have. After I finish this column, I'm going to call Mother Mary and hear her say:

Hi, stranger.

Now, consider that daughter Francesca has graduated from college and is living at home, temporarily. She's deciding what to do and where to do it, and sooner or later, she's going to fly the coop for good. I won't be able to say "pleasant dreams" to her anymore. I don't know how to prepare for that, and wouldn't try if I did. I'm just grateful for the time we have together.

And so, to me, that's the weird thing about Life in the Middle Ages. We are all of us, in some way, waiting to be left.

We exist in a state of emotional suspended animation.

It ain't easy, and it makes me wonder:

Aren't we really women "of an uncertain age?"

LOVE

Whenever Valentine's Day comes up, the newspaper, TV, and stores are full of heart-shaped candy boxes, roses, and jewelry for "that special someone." The holiday has become a celebration of romantic love, and that's great if you're in a romance or you're married, which is like having an automatic valentine.

But not everyone is so lucky.

There are plenty of people who aren't seeing someone right now, which is code for haven't had a date in 55 years. Like me. And that's okay, every day except Valentine's Day.

Single people feel like losers on Valentine's Day. They're left out of the hearts and candy. They become wallflowers at the party of life.

This is sad, and wrong. I think it's time to revisit the way we think about Valentine's Day. So welcome to another trademark

Scottoline time-to-change-things story, wherein my bossy and controlling nature works to my advantage, for once.

To begin, I did some research, and I learned that St. Valentine's Day was intended to celebrate a loving man, a priest so sweet, giving, and devout that he became a saint. Historically, his day had nothing to do with romance. In fact, it wasn't until the Middle Ages, when Geoffrey Chaucer wrote a poem entitled a *Parliament of Foules,* that St. Valentine's Day became associated with romantic love.

Aha! So the link between Valentine's Day and romance is pure fiction. Chaucer made it up, and trust me, he did it to move some poems. Sex sells. Romance novels are best-sellers for a reason, and even my books have sex scenes, which I write from memory.

And now I forget.

Given that the history of the holiday is so sketchy, I feel free to write on a clean slate. In other words, I can make it up, too.

And if you ask me, Valentine's Day is really about love. Not only romantic love, but also just plain love. And if you're not married or seeing someone, you can still have love in your life.

Observe.

In my case, I have tons of love in my life. I

love my kid, my family, and my friends. I love the people I work with. I love my readers. I love my dogs, cats, and pony. I love spaghetti. I love opera. I love books. I love Brad Pitt in *Legends of the Fall.*

In short, I love.

If I were going to improve on that maxim of Descartes, "I think, therefore I am," I'd say, "I love, therefore I am." Or instead of Pope's saying, "To err is human," I'd go with, "To love is human." Plus I agree completely with that great philosopher James Taylor, who tells us to "shower the people you love with love."

So I propose that, on Valentine's Day, we celebrate love. Shower the people you love with love. Don't take each other for granted. Recognize that we grow more valuable to each other as time passes, not less. Raise a glass to someone you love, in celebration of an emotion that powers our best intentions, leads to our greatest happiness, and gives us the stories of the world's greatest operas, movies, and novels.

In addition to *Gossip Girl.*

Now, there may be some of you reading this who have no one. Maybe you've lost someone, or they're far away, and you're left hiding in your house or apartment, waiting for Valentine's Day to pass.

Here's my advice to you:

Find the love in your life, because it's all around you. And if you can't find it, make it yourself.

Make love.

And by that, I don't mean match.com.

I mean, adopt a dog and love it. Buy it a pretty collar and walk it around the block. A cat works, too. Cats like pretty collars, even though they're too proud to say so. Or get a fish. There's no shame in love you can buy, even if it has scales. I don't think goldfish get enough credit. Not everybody can look good in orange.

Or read a book that everyone says is great. You'll find a story you love, and maybe an author. Or if you don't like to read, go see *Legends of the Fall.* You'll love Brad Pitt, whether you're a man or a woman.

And if none of that appeals to you, volunteer at a shelter or a hospital. Cook a meal for the parents at Ronald McDonald House, like a friend of mine did.

Because the thing about love is that we can't control whether we get it, but we can control whether we give it.

And each feels as good as the other.

Your heart doesn't know whether it's loving a man, a TV show, or a guppy. If your heart were that smart, it would be your brain.

All your heart knows is that it's full and happy, and you will feel alive and human.

And next time, you will have a wonderful Valentine's Day.

And, better yet, a wonderful life.

ACKNOWLEDGMENTS

Usually, in my novels, the Acknowledgments are the place where I step out of character, write in my own voice, get personal, and thank people whom readers may not know. But this time, the entire book is personal, and you've already met those who deserve my deepest thanks — my extraordinary mother Mary, brother Frank, and daughter Francesca.

And my father, Frank Scottoline.

And don't forget best friends, also extraordinary, Franca and Laura.

I love them all and am so grateful to each and every one of them for permitting me to take the stuff of our everyday lives and make it public. Not every author has such an understanding crew, but I am blessed in so many ways, in them. So thank you all so much.

This book wouldn't have been possible without the opportunity afforded me by the great people at *The Philadelphia Inquirer.* First, thanks to editor Sandy Clark, who helped me transition from 90,000 words to 900, every week. Weight loss has never been so much fun. Big thanks to publisher Brian Tierney, who has done so much for a city we both love, and thanks, too, Bill Marimow, Ed Mahlman, and Hilary Vadner.

Behind the scenes, too, is my wonderful agent Molly Friedrich, with her SWAT team of combination agents/cheerleaders/ therapists, Paul Cirone and Lucy Carson. Lucy is the girl genius who called this book a mix tape, which I stole gratefully. Thanks so much and lots of love for all you have done for me and my books, for so many years.

Big thanks and love to the amazing people at St. Martin's Press: John Sargent, Sally Richardson, Matt Baldacci, Matthew Shear, Jeff Capshew, Courtney Fischer, John Murphy, John Karle, and Mary Beth Roche, Laura Wilson, and the other great folks in audio. And above all, my terrific editor, Coach Jen Enderlin.

Finally, permit me a special thank-you to my favorite tea bags — Jen, Molly, Laura, and Franca. These women are extraordinary in so many ways, and they make me feel that I can be myself and say it all, out loud.

It's why they are not only great women but also great moms.

Thank you so much, ladies, for helping me find my own voice.

It's every woman's journey.

The employees of Thorndike Press hope you have enjoyed this Large Print book. All our Thorndike, Wheeler, and Kennebec Large Print titles are designed for easy reading, and all our books are made to last. Other Thorndike Press Large Print books are available at your library, through selected bookstores, or directly from us.

For information about titles, please call:
(800) 223-1244

or visit our Web site at:
http://gale.cengage.com/thorndike

To share your comments, please write:
Publisher
Thorndike Press
295 Kennedy Memorial Drive
Waterville, ME 04901